Jürgen Habermas

Modern European Thinkers
Series Editors: Anne Beech and David Castle

Over the past few decades, Anglo-American social science and humanities
have experienced an unprecedented interrogation, revision and strengthening
of their methodologies and theoretical underpinnings through the influence
of highly innovative scholarship from continental Europe. In the fields of
philosophy, post-structuralism, psychoanalysis, critical theory and beyond,
the works of a succession of pioneering writers have had revolutionary effects
on Anglo-American academia. However, much of this work is extremely
challenging, and some is hard or impossible to obtain in English translation.
This series provides clear and concise introductions to the ideas and work of
key European thinkers.

As well as being comprehensive, accessible introductory texts, the titles
in the 'Modern European Thinkers' series retain Pluto's characteristic radical
political slant, and critically evaluate leading theorists in terms of their
contribution to genuinely radical and progressive intellectual endeavour. And
while the series does explore the leading lights, it also looks beyond the big
names that have dominated theoretical debates to highlight the contribution
of extremely important but less well-known figures.

Also available

Alain Badiou
Jason Barker

Georges Bataille
Benjamin Noys

Jean Baudrillard
Mike Gane

Walter Benjamin
Esther Leslie

Pierre Bourdieu
Jeremy F. Lane

Gilles Deleuze
John Marks

André Gorz
Conrad Lodziak and Jeremy Tatman

Guy Hocquenghem
Bill Marshall

Julia Kristeva
Anne-Marie Smith

Slavoj Žižek
Ian Parker

Jürgen Habermas

Democracy and the Public Sphere

Luke Goode

Pluto Press

LONDON • ANN ARBOR, MI

First published 2005 by Pluto Press
345 Archway Road, London N6 5AA
and 839 Greene Street, Ann Arbor, MI 48106

www.plutobooks.com

British Library Cataloguing in Publication Data
A catalogue record for this book is available from the British Library

ISBN   0 7453 2089 9 hardback
ISBN   0 7453 2088 0 paperback

Goode, Luke, 1971–
    Jürgen Habermas : democracy and the public sphere / Luke Goode.
        p. cm. — (Modern European thinkers)
    Includes bibliographical references.
    ISBN 0–7453–2089–9 (hb) — ISBN 0–7453–2088–0 (pb)
  1. Habermas, Jürgen. Strukturwandel der Öffentlichkeit. 2. Sociology—Methodology.
3. Democracy. 4. Mass media—Political aspects. 5. Political participation. 6. Political
sociology. 7. Internet—Political aspects. I. Title. II. Series.
    HM585.G66 2005
    302.23—dc22
                                                                    2005014366

60543407

10   9   8   7   6   5   4   3   2   1

Designed and produced for Pluto Press by
Chase Publishing Services Ltd, Fortescue, Sidmouth, EX10 9QG, England
Typeset from disk by Stanford DTP Services, Northampton, England
Printed and bound in the European Union by
Antony Rowe Ltd, Chippenham and Eastbourne, England

Contents

Acknowledgements

There are many people – friends, colleagues, critics and inspirational teachers – who have helped to shape this book in one way or another. In particular, I would like to acknowledge the following people: Matt Connell, Simon Cross, Douglas Hoey, Conrad Lodziak, Steve Matthewman, Gabe Mythen, Nick Perry, Richard Ronald, Steve Sobol, Lloyd Spencer, Catherine Stones, Jeremy Tatman, Steve Taylor, John Tomlinson, Nabeel Zuberi. Jayne, Charis and Agatha have been invaluable sources of support, patience and distraction. Finally, I would like to acknowledge my old man who once made the mistake of lending me an intriguing little book entitled *The Structural Transformation of the Public Sphere*: this little book is dedicated to his memory.

Introduction

There is a paradox in the reception of the Habermasian idea of the public sphere. On the one hand, it seems like well-trodden territory. In fact, it is now increasingly dismissed as idealistic, Eurocentric and unwittingly patriarchal. On the other hand, it continues to be routinely invoked in debates around democracy, citizenship and communication. There's a certain parallel in the stubborn refusal of 'ideology' to disappear from the lexicon of social thought, despite the intellectual 'passing' of Marx, or the stickiness of the 'unconscious' long after the Freudians left the building. This book is motivated at least in part by a sense that when a key concept or intellectual figure is declared passé, the time is ripe for a reappraisal. What has Habermas contributed to current thinking? And if we want to understand the legacy of Habermasian thinking, we should at least try to churn up this well-trodden ground to see if there are any hidden valuables to be unearthed.

The book has several aims. First, it offers the reader an introduction to the concept of the public sphere as it has been developed by Habermas. Although it does not provide a comprehensive overview of every aspect of Habermas's critical theory, it does situate the idea of the public sphere, which occupied him early on in his career, in the context of subsequent developments in his thinking. Critical commentaries on Habermas have often treated the public sphere as a discrete topic. I hope to show that it remains fundamental to his entire intellectual project, even where it receives less explicit attention.

Second, I offer a critical but sympathetic reading of Habermas. Because I want to focus on sorting those insights that are most valuable in the context of contemporary debates from those that are not, I adopt what many may see as a skewed approach. I discuss a range of criticisms and secondary commentaries on Habermas, but I give most attention to those critics who share Habermas's concern with the problems of democracy, communication and citizenship. Unlike many commentaries, I do not devote a large amount of space to the great 'theory wars' that separate Habermas from opponents such as Jean-François Lyotard, Michel Foucault or Jacques Derrida, for whom Habermas is scarcely even asking the right questions. In taking this approach, I hope to be able to provide a productive 'internal critique' of Habermasian thinking. But, of course, there is also plenty of insight to be lost in such an approach. Moreover, though we should be wary of artificial distinctions, this book engages Habermas primarily as a social, political and communications theorist, more so than as a formal philosopher.

Third, I aim to turn the Habermasian concept of the public sphere outwards. As well as discussing what Habermas has said and what he may have meant by it, I try to suggest ways in which we might take the idea of the public sphere forward, intellectually and politically. Although the book takes only a few very tentative steps in this direction, it does make some suggestions on how the concept of the public sphere might be put to work in the future.

The first chapter looks closely at Habermas's classic work of historical study, *The Structural Transformation of the Public Sphere*. The chapter is an excavation *of* an excavation. Chapter 2 considers some of the critical responses that *Structural Transformation* has provoked and asks what we can learn from them. Chapter 3 looks at some of the subsequent theoretical manoeuvres undertaken by Habermas and asks how they might recast our understanding of the public sphere. The final two chapters focus on that task of turning the Habermasian public sphere outwards. Chapter 4 looks at the role of the media (both media institutions and media forms) in the discourse of the public sphere. It argues that *mediation*, and not merely *communication*, must be taken seriously when we are theorising the public sphere. In doing so, it touches on the significance of new media and 'digital culture'. Finally, Chapter 5 explores the concept of 'reflexivity' and argues that this must be at the core of a 'politics of the public sphere'.

1
Excavations: The History of a Concept

In this book I hope to make the case for seeing *The Structural Transformation of the Public Sphere* as a work that still resonates with some of the urgent questions facing the 'democratic project' today. In privileging this work and the category 'public sphere', I'm suggesting that if we want to enrich our grasp of the problems facing the democratic imagination, we would do well to read Habermas's later works through the lens of *Structural Transformation* and its key concerns. *Structural Transformation* invites us to reflect closely on the nature of public deliberation and the democratic process at a time when the rhetoric of 'citizenship' has become such common currency – especially, though not exclusively, in Western democracies – against a backdrop of striking developments: increasingly sophisticated political marketing techniques; changes in media culture that implicate the very institutions which aspire to connect citizens with the powerful; an ascendant politics of ethnicity and ethno-nationalism which can sometimes displace and sometimes appropriate the discourse of citizenship; and patterns of political behaviour, such as staggeringly low voting rates, which highlight widespread disaffection with the official institutions of democracy, especially in the younger generations.

A historicist reading of *Structural Transformation* could read off the present and future in terms of an unfolding historical dialectic: either a negative dialectic in which the potential for a truly democratic and rational public sphere has been irreversibly squandered, or a positive dialectic that gestures towards a radical–democratic endgame in which the rationality of the undemocratic bourgeois public sphere and the democracy of the irrational mass society might finally be reconciled. But what I propose instead is to read *Structural Transformation* as the sort of encounter between theory and history that offers a useful counterweight to the drift into abstraction characteristic of more recent critical theory. It is this kind of historically grounded attention to the evolution of discourses, practices and institutions that, I suggest, does more to energise and stimulate our thinking about democracy than either a *philosophically* abstract preoccupation with the relationship between law, morality and reason, or an *institutionally* abstract preoccupation with constitutional norms and human rights, both of which have been at the centre of the Habermasian project in recent years.

The point of *Structural Transformation* is *not* to provide a history to feed our nostalgic aspirations, and Habermas himself has never idealised the eighteenth-century public sphere to quite the degree that his critics have charged. Instead, it offers us a frame of reference which may help us to reflect on both the points of connection *and* the discontinuities between the past and our current predicament. Though as historiography it may not always pass muster with professional historians, scholars of social and political thought can find more in *Structural Transformation* than in any of Habermas's more recent works to expose the slippages between ambiguous, complex histories and virtuous ideals or grand theoretical systems. We start, then, with a survey of the main themes of *Structural Transformation*.

THE BOURGEOIS PUBLIC SPHERE

Under feudalism, Habermas reports, the 'public realm' existed not as a sphere of interaction and debate but merely of representation: aristocracy and nobility played out the symbolic dramas of majesty and highness before their subjects. To talk of a public realm is even misleading insofar as 'publicness', as a status attribute or performative mode, was more significant than spatial location.[1] The links between this 'representative publicness' and today's mass-mediated spectacles of public life are thin: it was simply staged performance *before* the people, not *on behalf* of a public. In fact, there was no 'public' as such, only public display. A distinct public realm and its corollary, a distinct private sphere, were all but absent. However, emergent forms of trade and finance capitalism – Habermas here focuses on Britain, France and Germany – and the eventual establishment of a 'civil society' underpinned by the ideology of 'private' autonomy, would eventually transform 'publicness' into something very different.

Long before feudalism was in its death throes, the increasing geographical reach and regularity of early capitalist trading set in train an expanding network of communications, primarily trade newsletters.[2] To begin with, the newsletters circulated among closed networks of merchants. This was not yet the rise of a print-based public culture. 'Publicness' was still the preserve of the feudal powers and it remained primarily oral, theatrical and immediate. By the sixteenth century, however, the European social landscape was changing rapidly and capitalist trade began to assume a foundational rather than adjunct role in economic and political life. Growing interdependence between an increasingly centralised state[3] and the merchant capitalists (the former securing the political and military force to underpin the expansion of foreign and domestic markets, the latter securing revenue for the former) signalled the beginnings of a novel sense of 'publicness'. 'The feudal powers, the Church, the prince, and the nobility, who were the carriers of the representative publicness, disintegrated in a process of polarisation':[4] the Reformation paved the way for the growing privatisation of religion; public authority assumed more bureaucratic dimensions (including a greater separation between parliament and judiciary); and the state budget enjoyed greater independence from the monarch's private holdings. The people were still merely subjects but the term 'public' now came to be associated with matters pertaining to an increasingly depersonalised state authority.[5] The publicness and significance of the noble and aristocratic courtly cultures began to diminish.

A complex relationship between economy and state emerged during the mercantilist phase. On the one hand, struggles over economic production and trade saw an increasingly confident 'private sphere' starting to erode the omnipotence of the state. A nascent bourgeoisie was carving out its independence and building a 'civil society' based on private commerce. But, under mercantilism, of course, economic affairs were a matter of intense public interest. The state authority depended on the fruits of private economic initiative and the fate of the bourgeoisie hung on the state's tax policies, legal statutes and military:

> Because, on the one hand, the society now confronting the state clearly separated a private domain from public authority and because, on the other hand, it turned the reproduction of life into something transcending the confines of private domestic authority and becoming a zone of public interest, that zone of administrative contact became 'critical' … in the sense that it provoked the critical judgment of a public making use of its reason.[6]

This 'critical reasoning' depended on the dissemination of printed information. For Habermas, the political, economic, cultural and technological developments of the press played a fundamental role: the modern conception of an active, reasoning 'public' – as distinct from a collection of 'subjects' – is unimaginable without them. The press emerged as an outgrowth of the increasing traffic in merchant newsletters. Already, under feudalism, these newsletters had 'unleashed the very elements within which this power structure would one day dissolve'.[7]

Habermas paints the second half of the seventeenth century as a critical period during which something approaching a publicly accessible 'press' emerged, feeding off and filtering the news conveyed in the private correspondences of the merchant capitalists.[8] This marked the emergence of regularised printed communication addressed to unspecified recipients. Of course, the 'audience' was largely confined to bourgeois and intellectual strata. But crucially, the press departed from the principle of immediacy: a piece of news was no longer a private affair, something of interest only to those whom it directly implicated, but was part of a larger communicative environment premised on a putative general interest. This 'general interest' was more than simply a novel ideological construct: it also reflected the very material forces which progressively eroded localised economic self-sufficiency and integrated the bourgeoisie (and, of course, their workers who were *not* generally privy to the new communication flows) into regional and national networks of interconnection and interdependency. They became expanded 'communities of fate', in other words,[9] or, to use Benedict Anderson's well-known formulation, 'imagined communities'.[10] This period saw the emergence of what were called 'political journals' (produced with increasing regularity until, eventually, daily publication became the norm) containing information on taxes, commodity prices, wars, foreign trade and the like.

For Habermas, two supply-side drivers were critically important for the growth of the press. First, news had become a commodity and there were economies of scale to be harnessed by producing news for expanded readerships. Second, state authorities rapidly cottoned on to the power of the printed word. As power migrated from the localism of the estates to a centralising state, print offered an efficient means of communicating decrees, proclamations, royal news and other symbols of authority across the territory.[11] But the effectiveness of this propaganda tool and the extent to which the medium provided a new forum for the old functions of 'representative publicness', ran up against obvious limits. On the demand side, there was a fundamental tension between the self-image of an emergent 'reasoning' public and the principle of rule by decree.[12] In mercantilism the state had set in train a 'peculiar ambivalence of public regulation and private initiative'.[13] In that liminal zone between the state and what would later emerge as 'civil society', the press did more to kindle than to smother the flames of bourgeois revolt.

By the early eighteenth century it had become commonplace for the pages of journals and periodicals to be taken up not simply with economic information and state propaganda, but with critical, openly opinionated articles: 'In the guise of so-called learned articles, critical reasoning made its way into the daily press.'[14] The press was implicitly critical because its operations challenged the interpretative duopoly of church and state. In the early phases such articles were less likely to attack the activities of state head-on than to plough an impressively independent line on literary, philosophical or pedagogic matters. (The early *Spectator*, for example, focused on the discussion of literature, morality and etiquette.) For this reason, Habermas identifies a bourgeois public sphere in the 'world of letters' as the precursor to a more directly political public sphere.

The precursory role that Habermas assigns to the literary public sphere suffers a certain ambiguity. After all, the literary public sphere Habermas portrays is, ostensibly, an eighteenth-century phenomenon, whilst the previous century is characterised by the emergence of a press more concerned with 'news' and information. In fact, *Structural Transformation* appears to assign the literary public sphere a precursory role on three levels. First, the seventeenth-century press did not, by and large, reflect the 'critical reasoning' Habermas reads into the eighteenth-century public sphere. Pages taken up with commodity prices, taxes, state announcements and so forth did not, of themselves, construct a 'reasoning public' critically reflecting upon matters of state. Second, to the extent that a *political* public sphere is linked to active struggles over the levers of state power, the eighteenth-century literary public sphere prefigures its political counterpart, at least insofar as the formal enfranchisement of the bourgeoisie serves as a yardstick. Finally, there is a synchronic consideration: in the idealistic self-image of the bourgeois public sphere, the literary public sphere is constituted as a 'pre-political' realm of self-clarification, a zone of freedom in which a putative 'humanity' or 'authentic' subjectivity could flourish, whose protection must become the *raison d'être* of a 'just' polity.

The literary public sphere spread beyond the pages of the printed press and beyond the restricted strata of the pedagogues and *philosophes*. 'Critical reasoning' occupied the proliferating coffee houses (especially in late seventeenth- and early eighteenth-century

England), the salons (especially in pre-revolutionary France) and the literary societies.[15] Of course, illiteracy and poverty excluded much of the rural and the property-less urban populations, and the literature that was energising the bourgeoisie specifically *addressed* the bourgeoisie in both form and content.[16] The literary public sphere, though less exclusionary than its political counterpart, was also gendered: whilst women played an active role in the salons that were attached to private households, their participation in circles convened in the coffee houses and other public spaces was heavily restricted.[17]

Emerging through the literature was a novel, individualised sense of selfhood. Richardson's *Pamela*, Rousseau's *La Nouvelle Héloïse* and Goethe's *Werthers Leiden* exemplified a literary culture increasingly concerned with self-disclosure. From the mid-eighteenth century onwards, 'there was no longer any holding back … [T]he rest of the century revelled and felt at ease in a terrain of subjectivity barely known at its beginning.'[18] The literary public sphere located this subjectivity in the private realms of intimacy. The bifurcation of the public and private has a historical precedent in ancient Greece. Here, however, the locus of humanity was the public *agora* itself, through the pursuit of timeless virtues through sport and oratory, whilst the household-slave economy confined the here-and-now of material necessity to the privacy of the *oikos*.[19]

The bourgeois public sphere imagined itself to comprise private people coming together as a public.[20] Power and domination were anathema to a sacrosanct selfhood: the public sphere wanted to wrest culture and its interpretation from authority structures corrupted by public power. This project idealististically evoked an erasure of status: as art and literature were commodified, they would assume intrinsic worth and cease to function as strategic tools of the old powers; and they would become, in principle, accessible to all.[21]

> The bourgeois public's critical public debate took place in principle without regard to all preexisting social and political rank and in accord with universal rules. These rules, because they remained strictly external to the individuals as such, secured space for the development of these individuals' interiority by literary means. These rules, because universally valid, secured a space for the individuated person; because they were objective, they secured a space for what was most subjective; because they were abstract, for what was most concrete.[22]

For Habermas, the bourgeois public sphere was, in principle, shaped by the values of egalitarian dialogue. Even on the printed page, key periodicals resorted to dialogical editorial formats in which letters to the editor were accorded special status.[23] Whilst 'truth' was there to be uncovered, the values of critical dialogue were meant to erode dogmatism: discourse should remain open to the equally valid claims of new participants and arguments; each site of discourse should see itself as part of a wider discursive environment.[24] Literary criticism adopted a new 'conversational' role as it sought to feed off and back into the discussions taking place in the coffee houses and literary societies.

The self-professed function of the *political* public sphere would be to secure the protection and integrity of the private sphere.[25] The bourgeoisie were adopting the mantle of the 'universal class' by asserting the meritocratic ideals of the free market. The process of conflating political (that is, bourgeois) and human (that is, universal) emancipation, which would become the target of Marx's critical energies, was underway. In the self-understanding of the bourgeois radicals, the political aspirations of their class were to be conceived in thoroughly negative terms: they did not seek a new division of power so much as a *neutralisation of power* to allow for the flowering of civil society.[26] The ideals of the political public sphere which granted participation rights *regardless* of status and privilege, could, in the eyes of the bourgeoisie, only be realised through cleansing privilege, constraint and public interference from the sphere of civil society, and through the development of a constitutional framework based on freedom of contract and laissez-faire trade policies.[27]

The bourgeoisie, claiming to stand as the locus of reason and justice, took on the task of challenging state secrecy.

> Historically, the polemical claim of this kind of rationality was developed, in conjunction with the critical public debate among private people, against the reliance of princely authority on secrets of state. Just as secrecy was supposed to serve the maintenance of sovereignty based on *voluntas*, so publicity was supposed to serve the promotion of legislation based on *ratio*.[28]

The press, of course, were to be the prime carriers of the new 'critical reasoning' in the political public sphere. Not surprisingly, Habermas devotes much attention to developments in Britain where, bitter conflicts over censorship notwithstanding,[29] the histories of press freedom and parliamentary reform have both earlier origins and a somewhat less volatile trajectory than in France or Germany. As Habermas points out, it is an irony of British history that we associate the rise of 'political journalism', a tradition dedicated to publicising and critiquing state activity, with the Tories during their protracted period of opposition and virtual exclusion from public office in the first half of the eighteenth century. If the Whigs brought the expansive economic interests of the bourgeoisie into Parliament, the Tories were pivotal in elevating the status of *public opinion*. They worked to establish the press as a 'fourth estate of the realm' willing to confront state authorities.[30] The traditional stand-offs between King and Parliament were being displaced by those between 'parties' of power and opposition. Henceforth, opposition parties, of whichever colour, would claim a moral high ground 'uncorrupted' by power. Increasingly, they could also appeal to 'public opinion' as a yardstick of legitimacy in political debate. 'Such occurrences', Habermas reminds us, 'must not be construed prematurely as a sign of a kind of rule of public opinion.'[31] But they signalled a moral and rhetorical evolution in the history of public opinion which would later be reflected structurally in the democratic reforms of the nineteenth century.

Habermas's attention to the British case is telling: that, in contrast to France, the early appeal to a newly elevated 'public opinion' came through conservative, aristocratically connected strata, resonates with the *formalistic* conception of democracy he has pursued throughout his career. At one level, Habermas cedes to the self-image of the eighteenth-century bourgeois public sphere the claim that bourgeois publicity does more than simply reflect a narrow, historically contingent class interest. However (and this is a paradox he does not address adequately), Habermas shows how the specific class interests (their opposition to economic liberalisation) of the British Tories made them only half-hearted champions of public opinion. The public, in their view (prefiguring twentieth-century models of democratic elitism), were not suitably equipped to deliberate on substantive matters of state but were, at least, well-placed to judge those in power on their integrity.

Habermas sketches some of the contrasts between developments in the political public spheres of Britain and the Continent. Limited space demands the briefest of summaries here. In Britain, a 150-year struggle, beginning with the Glorious Revolution, sees the press given new de facto and, eventually, constitutionally secured powers to make public the proceedings of Parliament. At the same time, various attempts are made to control and censor, including stamp taxes, which remain in place until the mid-nineteenth century. But they enjoy only mixed success.[32] '[B]esides the new, large daily newspapers like *The Times* (1785), other institutions of the public reflecting critically on political issues arose in these years ... [P]ublic meetings increased in size and frequency. Political associations too were formed in great numbers.'[33] By the end of the eighteenth century, 'loosely knit clubs' and unstable alliances had transformed themselves into parties with clear lines of demarcation and, for the first time, extra-parliamentary structures. 'Public opinion' was increasingly invoked by opposition and ministers alike. Finally, the extension of the franchise to the middle classes in 1832, and the publication of the first issue-based election manifesto, signalled the transformation of Parliament, 'for a long time the target of critical comment by public opinion, into the very organ of this public opinion'.[34]

By contrast, the French story is more staccato. Constitutional props, lacking in Britain, underpinned the proliferation of daily press and parliamentary factions after the Revolution. Yet they were also symptomatic of the precarious nature of the revolutionary public sphere.[35] Before the Revolution, strict censorship had made for a clandestine press, and subsequent constitutional settlements were punctuated by periods of terror. There was a lack, in all but name, of an assembly of estates suitable for reformation into a modern parliament, and a more deeply entrenched gulf between the bourgeoisie and nobility. In Germany, the growth of politically oriented reading societies and critical journals still met with 'the brutal reaction of the princes' at the end of the eighteenth century.[36] Such reaction, of course, attested to the growing critical strength of a 'bourgeois publicity' transforming the political landscape.

But Habermas does not simply document the rise of public opinion. He is also concerned with shifts in, and struggles over, the very meaning of 'public opinion'. In the prehistory of the phrase, 'opinion' harboured negative connotations. Deriving from the Latin *opinio* and associated with the Greek *doxa*, 'opinion' suggested judgment based on presumption rather than reason. A further usage linked the word to reputation or esteem. It lacked the fundamental features of critical reflection, validity or publicness which only came to the fore during the eighteenth century.[37] In the mid-seventeenth century, Hobbes serves as an unwitting signpost towards this later development. For Hobbes, living in the shadow of the Civil War, it was necessary to purge religious conviction from the purview of state authority.

Stripped of Hobbesian misanthropy, opinion might then rise above religious prejudice.[38] Later, Locke would explicitly elevate 'opinion' above prejudice but he did not claim for it a *public* or legislative role.[39] His view, radical at the time, was that opinion could form the basis for 'censure' against the weaknesses and misdemeanours of public authority.

Habermas contends that the conjoining of 'public' and 'opinion' is at least partly an innovation of the British Tories (and oppositional Whigs) who crafted the modern art of opposition in their appeals to a 'sense of the people' or a 'public spirit'.[40] Yet 'opinion' still evoked immediacy and it befell the political class (who were not yet, strictly speaking, 'representatives') to transform it into reason and judgment. Later that century, Burke's theory of 'virtual representation' articulated a shift from 'public spirit' to 'public opinion'. 'The opinion of the public that put its reason to use was no longer just opinion; it did not arise from mere inclination but from private reflection upon public affairs and from their public discussion.'[41] Opinion was losing its association with immediacy in favour of 'critical reflection'.

In revolutionary France, by contrast, Rousseau's 'public opinion' evoked the instinctual *bon sens* of 'the people' against the physiocrats who saw critical reflection as the foundation stone of loyalty. The physiocratic view of the 'enlightened monarch' entailed public debate without democracy. By contrast,

> Rousseau wanted democracy without public debate ... However, the Revolution itself combined the two sundered functions of public opinion, the critical and the legislative. The Constitution of 1791 joined the principle of popular sovereignty with that of the parliamentary constitutional state, which provided a constitutional guarantee for a public sphere as an element in the political realm. The French concept of public opinion was radicalised compared to the British notion.[42]

In Germany, the precise term 'public opinion' (*Öffentliche Meinung*) entered common parlance somewhat later. But Kant's 'principle of publicity' is critical for Habermas. Kant articulated the self-image of a critical public sphere in terms of subordinating politics to morality. Morality, immanent in the laws of a self-regulating civil society, could not (contra Hobbes) be 'demoted to the status of politically inconsequential ethical preference'.[43] The public sphere, to that extent, was to function as a bridge between the civil and political realms. The principle of publicity underpinning the public sphere appealed to a public use of reason, free of manipulation and coercion: a key virtue was thinking for one's self publicly, that is, as a member of humanity and not as a private individual.[44] The public should take their lead from the philosophers engaged in 'pure' reasoning, and '[e]ach person was called to be a "publicist", a scholar "whose writings speak to his public, the world"'.[45] 'Autonomy' is a prerequisite for participation in the Kantian republic: 'Only property-owning private people were admitted to a public engaged in critical political debate, for their autonomy was rooted in the sphere of commodity exchange and hence was joined to the interest in its preservation as a private sphere.'[46] Harmonious social relations would be possible because a free civil society would bring about a cosmopolitan consciousness and the contradiction between 'private vices' and 'public virtues' would be resolved. For everyone who had achieved the requisite autonomy, private aspirations (the maintenance of a 'free civil society') coincided with the aspirations of all who joined him in the public sphere of deliberation. A person who is 'his own master' serves only himself and, by extension, 'the commonwealth' of all persons, including those who are not yet capable of full citizenship but who implicitly share an interest in the renewal of a civil society which grants them equal chances of membership, regardless of status: 'the property-less were not citizens at all, but persons who with talent, industry, and luck some day might be able to attain that status'.[47] For Kant, the role of public deliberation is not to generate consensus or compromise, for 'pure reasoning' rather than dialogue would *reveal* the truth of things; instead, public deliberation, under the guidance of the scholars, provided something of a training in the art of 'thinking for oneself' and a continual reminder to think one's thoughts in the context of the universal 'public'. This early encounter with Kant is significant, for Habermas's entire oeuvre bears the imprint of Kantian thinking: he follows Kant in developing a universalist framework, though he substitutes the monologic conceit of 'pure reasoning' for the rule of dialogue and open-ended argumentation; and he favours Kant's model of a 'reasoning' public over Rousseau's 'common sense', though he is only interested in a republicanism that can accommodate liberalism's concern for the rights of the individual.[48]

But Habermas also lives in the shadows of Hegel and Marx who both abhorred such abstract reasoning. The Kantian system contained a debilitating impasse: a perfectly 'free' civil society (the 'juridical condition'), the necessary foundation of the 'condition of autonomy', had never existed in reality. Act two of the narrative sees Habermas focus on those dynamics which, rather than bringing history into line with the Kantian ideal, served only to transform both the institutional contours and self-image of the political public sphere.

THE FALL OF THE BOURGEOIS PUBLIC SPHERE

For Hegel, the intractable problems of privilege and conflict in civil society destroyed the universalism and permanence to which 'public opinion' could lay claim in the Kantian system. With Hegel, public opinion 'no longer retained a basis of unity and truth; it degenerated to the level of a subjective opining of the many'.[49] Politics could not be subsumed by an abstract 'universal morality'. The state is compelled to intervene in an unruly civil society. Yet, in standing above public opinion, the state could in principle unify civil society: it could become an embodiment of the Zeitgeist in which a populace craving spirit, rather than abstract morality, would find meaning. In the Hegelian system, then, public opinion is paradoxically respected *and* despised as it both reflects and threatens to dissolve a national ethos.[50] For Habermas, Hegel demotes the public sphere to a 'means of education', motivation and assembly for an otherwise entropic public opinion.[51]

Marx, like Hegel, saw civil society characterised by intractable contradictions rather than a latent harmony of interests but, as is well known, this ultimately led him down a very different path. Whilst the universal ideals of the bourgeois revolutions served to conceal their partial realisation, Hegel's glorification of the Prussian estates-based constitution looked to Marx like a futile attempt to rewind the emancipatory energies unleashed by the revolutions.[52] For Hegel, the bourgeois public sphere had, in assuming legislative functions, become *too* public. For Marx, by contrast, it was *not public enough*. Marx's statement on the German bourgeoisie in 1844 neatly encapsulates this perspective:

> It is not radical revolution or universal human emancipation which is a utopian dream for Germany; it is the partial, merely political revolution, the revolution which leaves the pillars of the building standing. What is the basis of a partial and merely political revolution? Its basis is the fact that one part of civil society emancipates itself and attains universal domination, that one particular class undertakes from its particular situation the universal emancipation of society. This class liberates the whole of society, but only

on the condition that the whole of society finds itself in the same situation as this class, e.g. possesses or can easily acquire money and education.[53]

Workers, eventually seeing through the fog of the 'free market' their real conditions of alienation and exploitation, would at last carry forward the programme of a truly universal emancipation. Habermas summarises the socialistic model of the public spheres as follows:

> From the dialectic immanent in the bourgeois public sphere Marx derived the socialist consequences of a counter-model in which the classical relationship between the public sphere and the private was peculiarly reversed. In this counter-model, criticism and control by the public were extended to that portion of the private sphere of civil society which had been granted to private persons by virtue of their power of control over the means of production … According to this new model … [p]rivate persons came to be the private persons of a public rather than a public of private persons … [T]he public sphere no longer linked a society of property-owning private persons with the state. Rather, the autonomous public … secured for itself … a sphere of personal freedom, leisure, and freedom of movement. In this sphere, the informal and personal interactions of human beings with one another would have been emancipated for the first time from the constraints of social labor … and become really 'private'.[54]

But Marx, like Hegel, laboured under a misguided historicism. Neither foresaw the changes which both the public sphere itself and, indeed, the critical discourses of 'public opinion' would undergo. As the nineteenth century progressed, the political public sphere became an arena whose consensually oriented self-image began to give way to one concerned with conflict management and the *division* rather than dissolution of power: compromise between interest groups and factions became the guiding principle.[55] The writings of J.S. Mill and Alexis de Tocqueville reflected this transformation: 'With liberalism … the bourgeois self-interpretation of the public sphere abandoned the form of a philosophy of history in favor of a common sense meliorism – it became "realistic".'[56]

Nineteenth-century liberals observed a public sphere expanding through the growth of press outlets and the spread of literacy and through the rise of working class, women's suffrage and, beyond Europe, anti-slavery movements. They also witnessed more and more conflict within the capitalist class itself. Marx notwithstanding, 'Electoral reform was the topic of the nineteenth century: no longer the principle of publicity as such ... but of the enlargement of the public ... The self-thematisation of public opinion subsided.'[57] It also became important for nineteenth-century liberalism to emphasise the dangers of public opinion and the importance of defending individual liberties from the tyranny of the majority.[58] The concerns of Mill and de Tocqueville were, Habermas points out, double-sided. Whilst lamenting a 'tyrannical' aspect to public opinion, they also criticised the excessive bureaucratisation and centralisation of state power, which developed rapidly during the transition towards a more intensively organised (interventionist) phase of capitalism. Whilst chiding them for their 'reactionary politics',[59] Habermas praises their sense of the changing relationship between the state and the political public sphere, one far more prescient than either the bourgeois or Marxian models:

> Two tendencies dialectically related to each other indicated a breakdown of the public sphere. While it penetrated more spheres of society, it simultaneously lost its political function, namely: that of subjecting the affairs that it had made public to the control of a critical public.[60]

We might, then, surmise that, if nineteenth-century society saw democracy spread more widely, then it also saw it spread more thinly. But that glosses over some complexities. The fate of the political public sphere under organised capitalism is characterised by Habermas as a process of 'refeudalisation', where 'the distinction "public" and "private" could [no longer] be usefully applied'.[61]

The transition towards organised capitalism involved the interlocking of state and society. 'Society' strengthens its grip on state power. But instead of a convergence of interests between civil society and the state, the coherence of civil society itself is progressively eroded as market 'imperfections' become endemic crises. 'Processes of concentration and crisis pulled the veil of an exchange of equivalents off the antagonistic structure of society.'[62] With organised private interest groups clamouring for the levers of state power, some demanding protectionism and others liberalisation, the politicisation of civil society intensifies.[63] Working-class agitation also intensifies this politicisation and ultimately results not, as Marx anticipated, in the dissolution of capitalism, but in expanded suffrage, Keynsian redistributive measures, the 'publification' of contractual law and collective wage-bargaining processes, and welfarism. Zones of activity emerged that were, strictly speaking, neither private nor public:

the 'public sector' related in a privatised manner towards 'clients' (individuals and corporations) and employees whilst operating under the banner of a 'public interest'.[64]

Against the bourgeois ideal, the very term 'public interest' was now assumed to reflect compromise and negotiation between antagonistic private interests. However, the point is not simply that the public sphere would no longer preoccupy itself primarily with uncovering a 'natural' coincidence between private and universal interests (and the ways in which this avenue was kept open, such as in discourses of nationalism, are lamentably absent from the purview of *Structural Transformation*). The continuity of the term 'private interest' between the bourgeois and post-bourgeois public spheres actually obscures a critical discontinuity central to Habermas's thesis, namely in the constitution of 'privacy' itself. What is at stake is the way in which private interests, as units of public opinion, were thought to be formed.

In the bourgeois model, the 'private' realm consisted in the intimate, familial sphere and the economic realm of the capitalist market place. The two components, one the precondition of the other, were both based on the ideals of autonomy and subjective freedom. In the self-image of an expanding, post-bourgeois public sphere, the economic realm and the domestic sphere became unhinged from one another. For the large majority of those who now qualified as citizens, the economic realm consisted not in capitalistic enterprise and the free deployment of private property, but in an objectified 'world of work'.[65] Complex new class configurations emerged with the rise of managerialism, dispersed shareholdings, and heavily unionised occupational sectors, eclipsing the binary opposition between property owner and wage labourer. Whilst the economy became more intensively politicised, the realm of 'private' freedoms began to close in on its contemporary associations with family life, intimacy and leisure.

Under liberal capitalism, bourgeois family life was supposedly set free from the realm of material production. But that autonomy was critically dependent on the economic success of the head of household.[66] Under organised capitalism, though, family life took on a different relationship to the economic realm. The family began to give way to the individual as the basic economic unit. The risks associated with the economic realm become more individualised and simultaneously softened in the context of welfarism. The welfare state did not, of course, simply bypass the family unit. To the present day, in fact, policies relating to welfare payments, tax, state education and the like, tend to invoke the nuclear family as the social norm. But welfarism also hailed the *individual* to an unprecedented degree: 'Against the so-called basic needs, which the bourgeois family once had to bear as a private risk, the individual family member today is publicly protected.'[67] A *culture* of welfarism, underscored by both state and non-state institutions, reached into domains of social reproduction that were once the preserve of the family: social services, relationship counselling, therapeutic services and proliferating channels of guidance on child rearing, diet, lifestyle and the like.

But the implications for changing public–private relations are complex. The domestic sphere became a 'hollowed out' realm of privacy[68] making way for an increasingly inward-looking privacy focused on leisure, consumption and lifestyle (a syndrome Habermas would later refer to as 'privatism').[69] Habermas, in this early work, calls these newfound private freedoms 'illusory'.[70] The divorce between public and private life was in fact one-sided and what developed was the 'the direct onslaught of extrafamilial authorities upon the individual'.[71] In a powerful turn of phrase, Habermas speaks of a 'floodlit privacy'.[72] Risking metaphorical excess, we might say that what Habermas laments is a society lacking the mirrors required either to shine the lights back on those institutions or to reflect adequately upon itself. In the bourgeois model, the political public sphere aspired to the former and the literary public sphere the latter and both were of a piece. But the reception of cultural products had now degenerated into a mere aspect of the 'noncommital use of leisure time'.[73] A culture *debating* public had, according to Habermas, been displaced by a culture *consuming* public.

A public sphere evolving 'from the very heart of the private sphere itself' no longer existed even as an aspiration:

> Bourgeois culture was not mere ideology. The rational–critical debate of private people in the salons, clubs, and reading societies was not directly subject to the cycle of production and consumption, that is, to the dictates of life's necessities. Even in its merely literary form ... it possessed instead a 'political' character in the Greek sense of being emancipated from the constraints of survival requirements. It was for these reasons alone the idea that later degenerated into mere ideology (namely: humanity) could develop at all. The identification of the property owner with the natural person, with the human being as such, presupposed a separation inside the private realm between, on the one hand, affairs that private people pursued individually

each in the interests of the reproduction of his own life and, on the other hand, the sort of action that united people into a public.[74]

This passage is helpful in clarifying Habermas's arguments. The ideological nature of eighteenth-century bourgeois universalism is indisputable. Yet the bourgeois public sphere could be more than *mere* ideology precisely *because* of the structural dominance of the bourgeoisie: to use the Aristotelian distinction, once favoured by Marx, the bourgeois public sphere could imagine itself to exist in the 'realm of freedom', rather than the 'realm of necessity'. The same could not be said for a majority of citizens in the post-bourgeois public sphere. Habermas, echoing the views of his Frankfurt School predecessors, treats the domain of 'leisure' less as a realm of freedom than as a recuperative and compensatory necessity shaped by the onerous demands of the world of work; for the most part leisure, in Adorno's phrase,[75] is a 'mere appendage of work', an extension of worker dependency. Whilst the 'leisure' enjoyed by the bourgeoisie stood at least at arm's length from questions of survival, leisure in the post-bourgeois world lacked the capacity 'to constitute a world emancipated from the immediate constraints of survival needs'.[76] The foundations of an autonomous realm of reflection and debate were lacking. Urban and suburban lifestyles were eroding the integrity of both privacy and publicity, and the solitary act of reading and the sociability of public debate, once symbiotic, were imploding into the television-dominated living room.[77] The frenetic pace of modern life didn't lend itself to critical reasoning. Neither, moreover, did the evolving mass media and cultural industries, for whom Habermas reserves much of his contempt.

Habermas's impassioned critique of the twentieth-century mass media and cultural industries is provocative and a little less than coherent. The reader is left to untangle the twin threads of sweeping polemic and more nuanced critique which enjoy an uneasy coexistence. I shall attempt, very briefly, to do a little unpicking here. Twentieth-century mass culture is drawn, for Habermas, towards a lowest common denominator. As the public sphere expands, the complexity of cultural products is lowered to make them more readily saleable: individuals do not have to raise their own levels of understanding and reflection to meet the requirements of the cultural supply.[78] Intellectuals, critics and the avant-garde become alienated and aloof from this homogenising mass.[79] This depiction, Habermas assures us, does not amount to elitism: what he laments is not the expansion of the 'public' per se but the way in which the untrammelled commercialism of mass culture congeals into tried and tested formulae. It favours the palatable immediacy of human-interest stories over complex processes, whilst fostering a facile intimacy. The complex characters and narratives of modern literature give way to advice columns, emotions laid bare, 'real life' stories, with 'real people' – celebrities and 'ordinary' folk – we can swiftly identify with: quite possibly Habermas would see the recent glut of cheap, high-rating 'reality TV' programmes as the apex of this culture of immediacy. Mass culture deprives audiences of the space to carry out psychological work for themselves: it takes on all their emotional needs and problems directly for them. The intimacy is 'illusory', though, precisely because this personal immediacy is handed down in depersonalised form – the psychological guidance is administered, en masse, in formulaic fashion: Habermas would likely see the bespoke 'interactivities' of today's digital mediascape as the latest achievement of this 'administered individualisation' (see Chapter 4).

To put it in McLuhanite terms (though Marshall McLuhan was much more approving), there is an implosion of the public and the private. Private life is publicised and public life is simultaneously privatised as public figures (stars, politicians and the like) are fed to us as predigested chunks of biography and psychological profile.[80] Debate and discussion of cultural goods, though increasingly 'unnecessary', hasn't been altogether killed off. But, like the cultural goods themselves, debate has become administered, carried out within the confines of professional media spaces, to a set of predefined rules and generic conventions: it serves as a 'tranquilising substitute for action'.[81]

Whilst the *commodification* of cultural supply is what troubles Habermas most in *Structural Transformation*, there is undoubtedly a thinly veiled but less than reasoned technophobia at play. Habermas's print-centric bias comes to the fore when he charges the new broadcast media with discouraging distanced reflection or extended discussion.[82] The relentless and frenetic churnings of radio and television are the main culprits.[83] Habermas has since conceded that his analysis was one-sided and that empirical research on media reception since he wrote *Structural Transformation* has increasingly problematised the assumptions of audience passivity;[84] on the other hand, however, recent remarks[85] suggest that Habermas has neither renounced nor properly qualified his logocentric antipathy towards the audio-visual media. The problem is *not* that Habermas dislikes mediated communication per se. As we have seen, he fears the *immediacy* of electronic media and favours the distance and space afforded by print culture as a complement to speech-based argumentation. But what he fails to emphasise adequately is just how precarious these distinctions are: the spoken word itself is always already mediated through embodiment; and the printed word does not *necessarily* afford more space and distance than electronic media – compare the scatter-gun temporality of the daily press with the reflective longitude afforded a television documentary researched and produced over months or years. The distinctions break down rapidly on examination and we shall have cause to revisit these problems later in the book.

There is a more compelling line of argument in *Structural Transformation*. Innovations in media technology (telegraphy, wireless broadcasting, print processes and so forth) had important economic consequences. They demanded high infrastructural outlay, which favoured larger and larger markets and a low 'elasticity of supply' – the introduction of television, for example, was (until recently) only economically viable on a truly mass scale.[86] But rather than developing this, Habermas focuses on the more general question of commodification, and his arguments demand some unravelling.

Habermas's narrative of the commodification of culture only partly echoes that of the Frankfurt School. Unlike Adorno and Horkheimer (and more like Walter Benjamin), he paints the early phase of commodification during the eighteenth century as a progressive, democratising force. At what point, then, does commodification become the villain of the piece? The answer, Habermas suggests, lies in 'rigorously distinguishing' between different functions of commodification. In the bourgeois model, commodification impacted only on distribution: it helped to uncouple culture from status by making it available to anyone who could afford it. It did not, however, drive the content.[87] The same cannot be said of the twentieth century:

> To the degree that culture became a commodity not only in form but also in content, it was emptied of elements whose appreciation required a certain amount of training – whereby the 'accomplished' appropriation once again heightened the appreciative ability itself. It was not merely standardisation as such that established an inverse relationship between the commercialisation of cultural goods and their complexity, but that special preparation of products that made them consumption-ready, which is to say, guaranteed

> an enjoyment without being tied to stringent presuppositions. Of course, such enjoyment is also entirely inconsequential ... [M]ass culture leaves no lasting trace; it affords a kind of experience which is not cumulative but regressive.[88]

But, at the very least, Habermas would have to relativise this tale of two commodifications in order to make it convincing. Even when maximum profit was not the *raison d'être* of the cultural industries – Habermas points out, for example, that for eighteenth-century literary journals a degree of loss-making was the norm[89] – it is hard to accept that content somehow remained utterly untainted by the logic of the market or that cultural producers could ever proceed merrily without any regard for commercial success. Habermas cites the mass production of what we now call 'paperback classics': this, he suggests, is the contemporary exception that proves the rule because market logic broadens distribution and access without damaging the integrity of the cultural product.[90] But this is a flawed argument: the mass appeal of particular 'classics' is what makes large, cheap print runs of some (and not other) titles economically viable. The mischievous response would be to ask Habermas to wander down the bookshop aisles containing all the abridged and audio editions of the 'classics' and invite him to comment on the integrity of the content. But the real point is that commodification has manifold and potentially ambivalent consequences for the cultural public sphere. It can improve access when economies of scale and competition lower costs, but it can also lead to the cultural industries policing supply, keeping costs high and excluding the less well-off; it can undermine elitism by rendering content responsive to the tastes and experiences of 'ordinary' folk, but it can also work to silence marginal and innovative forms whose market appeal is anything less than calculable (the recent popularisation of opera embodies these ambivalent tendencies). It's simply untenable and unhelpful to claim that the Penguin edition of Jane Austen and the Mills and Boon book signify two distinct modes of commodification: analysis of the contemporary cultural public sphere must instead be attuned to the consistently ambivalent potentials of commodification, even where we suspect the darker consequences to be in ascendancy.

With this in mind, we can now return to the basic kernel of Habermas's thesis: namely, that the mutually reinforcing tendencies of a citizenry bereft of space and time, and a cultural 'market place' which reduces the citizen to a ratings, box-office or circulation statistic, have all but dissolved the image of a critical public sphere; a sense of culture as 'political' by virtue of being an end-in-itself for producer and recipient alike has faded; so too have the symbiotic relations between the public and the private, and between the cultural and political public spheres. For Habermas, it is not the fact that state and society have become interlocked per se that erodes the principle of critical publicity. What matters is that this process erodes the old institutional bases of critical publicity without supplying new ones.[91] On the one hand, institutions of society (private interest groups, political parties and the like) become *part of* the state power structure. On the other hand, the state (and the culture of welfarism more generally) has reached into once private spheres of society with ambivalent consequences.

In classical liberalism, the parliamentary legislature, representing public opinion, mediates between competing private interests and executive authority. But the expansion of state activity exceeds the capacities of parliamentary process. Parliament becomes a cumbersome bottleneck in need of containment. It increasingly resembles a rubber-stamping committee: 'The process of the politically relevant exercise and equilibration of power now takes place directly between the private bureaucracies, special-interest associations, parties, and public administration.'[92] That's not to say that Parliament was entirely stripped of *symbolic* significance, especially as organised capitalism initiated such a visible expansion of state activity. (Since the 1980s, however, 'disorganised capitalism' has ushered in a much less visible expansion of state activity, obfuscated by a neo-liberal mythology of 'rolling back the state'.) But parties of government and opposition have generally been complicit in what Claus Offe has called the 'separation of form and content' in parliamentary democracies.[93] Parliamentary 'debate' became increasingly subjected to techniques of stage management. Internal party debate was similarly disciplined as increasingly defensive 'catch-all' parties scrapped over the votes of unaffiliated and apolitical citizens.[94]

During the twentieth century, then, Habermas sees a tragic trade-off unfolding. The expansion of democracy has come at the cost of its continual degradation. Where the bourgeois model conceived the act of voting merely as a necessary conclusion – a 'guillotine' – imposed on drawn-out processes of deliberation, today's 'plebiscitary' democracy is content to accept voting and democratic participation as synonymous (which is why low electoral turnouts are treated as the most scandalous indicators of the state of democracy). The number of plebiscites (including opinion polls and media vox pops as well as formal ballots) and the number of people at liberty to participate in them has been dramatically expanded. Moreover, today's plebiscitary culture does routinely acknowledge the problem of the ill-informed citizen, even if opinion polls and focus groups are indifferent to it. It's widely agreed that citizens should be aware of the propositions and beliefs underpinning each option on the ballot paper before they exercise their choice. But the governing logic here is not that of the public sphere: today's ethic of good citizenship does not demand that our opinions are 'tested out' in the argumentative crossfire of the coffee house or, for that matter, the Internet discussion group. Rather, the governing logic is that of the market: the analogy is the educated consumer who, before plucking goods from the supermarket shelf, carefully considers the range of choices on offer and the cases that competing corporations make for their products. 'Citizens relate to the state not primarily through political participation but by adopting a general attitude of demand.'[95]

If a lack of widespread participation in political debate renders the political public sphere more intensively mediated in one sense (politics is something you read *about*, *see* on the television and make yes/no responses *to*, not something you *do*), then it is rendered more *immediate* in another sense: the political public sphere is taken up almost entirely with the relationship between lay individuals and professional politicians vying to win their acclaim. Peer-to-peer public debate becomes an increasingly marginal practice.[96] Habermas does not claim that there is no longer any horizontal political debate to speak of, but that such debate is rarely *public*: 'the political discussions are for the most part confined to in-groups, to family, friends, and neighbors who generate a rather homogeneous climate of opinion anyway'.[97]

For Habermas, the 'public sphere' has become merely the aggregate of individualised preferences, an administrative variable brought into the circuit of power only when its presence is functionally required: 'Today occasions for identification have to be created – the public sphere has to be "made", it is not "there" anymore.'[98] In this context, Habermas talks of a shift away from the 'critical publicity' that underpinned the bourgeois model, towards that of 'manipulative publicity'. Where *public* deliberation provides a bulwark against prejudice, reactionism and parochial perspective, opinion in late capitalism has been reduced to a 'mood-dependent inclination'[99] more amenable to the symbolic push and pull of the publicity industries.

> In the end an opinion no longer even needs to be capable of verbalisation; it embraces not only any habit that finds expression in some kind of notion – the kind of opinion shaped by religion, custom, mores and simple 'prejudice' against which public opinion was called in as a critical standard in the eighteenth century – but simply all modes of behaviour.[100]

What drives much of Habermas's writing after *Structural Transformation* is precisely the goal of showing how this trade-off between democratic expansion and degradation might be conceived as something other than fateful tragedy.

CRITICAL PUBLICITY AND LATE CAPITALISM

The first tentative steps towards this 'reconstructive turn' are, however, taken in the closing pages of *Structural Transformation*. Though Habermas has no desire to see the promises of the bourgeois model redeemed in full – such hopes would be both unrealistic and dangerous – he does ponder on the possibilities for a renaissance of critical publicity within late capitalist democracies.

In the first instance, if the bourgeois model of critical publicity is to prove relevant to late capitalism then the state must be accorded a different role from that of the liberal phase. The altered scope of state activity demands an increase in critical publicity and scrutiny. To narrowly conceive of parliament as *the* public sphere writ large, corralling public opinion into a singular arena, would be to support an atrophied model of democracy. The changed scope of state activity is not to be lamented, but does demand new thinking on the ways in which it can be exposed to critical publicity.[101]

Apart from the dangers of narrowing the methods and scope of deliberation, to privilege Parliament is to reinforce a monocentric model of power which is unrealistic and regressive. Critical publicity, according to Habermas, must also be extended to those agencies (special-interest groups, corporations, professional associations, parties and so forth) which interact with the state: '

> Not only organs of state but all institutions that are publicistically influential in the political public sphere have been bound to publicity because the process in which societal power is transformed into political power is as

much in need of criticism and control as the legitimate exercise of political domination over society.[102]

Moreover, it would be dangerous to overlook those agencies which, whilst not accruing any direct political power, nevertheless influence the political process. Whatever 'public interest' credentials accrue, for example, to a media institution or campaign group, such organisations cannot legitimately stand aloof from the obligations of critical publicity. In other words, institutions that claim to be institutions *of* the public sphere must, themselves, be opened up to the critical scrutiny of a wider public sphere: Habermas, then, advocates a *reflexive publicity*. As long as public spheres operate above the heads of consumers and not in interaction with a critically debating public, they remain sorely lacking *as* public spheres. Politically relevant institutions

> must institutionally permit an intraparty or intra-association democracy – to allow for unhampered communication and public rational–critical debate. In addition, by making the internal affairs of the parties and special-interest associations public, the linkage between such an intraorganisational public sphere and the public sphere of the entire public has to be assured. Finally, the activities of the organisations themselves – their pressure on the state apparatus and their use of power against one another, as well as the manifold relations of dependency and of economic intertwining – need a far-reaching publicity. This would include, for instance, requiring that the organisations provide the public with information concerning the source and deployment of their financial means.[103]

Habermas's fragmentary remarks betray a rather pained ambivalence rather than a nostalgic attitude towards the bourgeois model and its idealised separation of the public and the private. On the one hand, if public authority can be understood realistically only as the outcome of conflicting 'private' interests (in which the so-called 'public sector' is also implicated), so the reverse is true: the 'private sphere' of civil society does, and indeed must, bear the imprint of public intervention. The bourgeois model cannot live up to its own ideals of universality and equality of participation by reference to merely de jure, that is, negative guarantees:

> [T]he formation of a public opinion in the strict sense is not effectively secured by the mere fact that anyone can freely utter his opinion and put

out a newspaper. The public is no longer composed of persons formally and materially on equal footing.[104]

Certainly Habermas declines to analyse extant and potential policy measures to address these inequalities. (Such indeterminacy is a source of frustration to many readers and commentators but also helps to keep *Structural Transformation* relevant and thought-provoking some decades later.) But the baseline argument remains that questions of democracy cannot be sheared off from questions of social inequality. (I explore this issue further in Chapter 2.) On the other hand, Habermas does not want to see the distinction between the public and the private extinguished altogether. He continues to value the idea of a space of reflection and clarification which feeds off and into *but is not governed by* the public sphere. But this discourse of private autonomy – what it means and whose interests it serves – is a vexed one: 'privacy' can shield manipulative power relations within the domestic sphere, for example, just as it can empower individuals to pursue their own life projects without public interference. Habermas's notion of privacy remains unsatisfactorily vague and I try to tease this issue out more satisfactorily in the following chapter.

Structural Transformation scarcely affords more clarity when it comes to the institutional dimensions of a reconstructed public sphere. For here Habermas is concerned less with imagining new political institutions as such as he is with the conscious and progressive application of the principle of critical publicity to existing institutions: parties, unions, extra-parliamentary decision-making spheres, media, special interest groups and so forth. The downside to this is an implicit conservatism: the focus is more on reforming and renewing extant institutions than it is on imagining new ones. I shall argue in later chapters that this conservatism rears its head even more strongly in Habermas's recent work on constitutionalism. But, by and large, Habermas has always been less concerned with the question of how radically we should rethink the *institutions* of democracy and the public sphere than with developing frameworks which can help us to evaluate the strengths and weaknesses of particular institutions. This formalistic orientation was already showing through even in *Structural Transformation*, his most concrete, historical investigation, in which he sketches some basic democratic values that prefigure his more recent ideas around 'discourse ethics'.

Public spheres must be judged according to their inclusivity: critical attention must focus on the ways in which particular groups or individuals are marginalised. It is, of course, in keeping with the norms and expectations of a democratic society that associations and organisations exist which comprise people of similar interests, opinions and backgrounds. But membership of and participation in such groups should not be conditional on ascriptive markers of status, such as wealth or ethnicity. Even then, it's only when their internal procedures are available for scrutiny by a broadly conceived, pluralistic public domain that they make a positive contribution to a reconstructed public sphere:

> The public sphere commandeered by societal organisations and that under the pressure of collective private interests has been drawn into the purview of power can perform functions of political critique and control, beyond mere participation in political compromises, only to the extent that it is itself radically subjected to the requirements of publicity, that is to say, that it again becomes a public sphere in the strict sense.[105]

And critical publicity implies the development of procedural norms governing internal and external relations, which give due weight to the principle of *open* dialogue in which nothing and no one is off limits. Such straightforward idealism will always exist in tension with both pragmatic considerations (how to get things done in the time available) and ethical considerations (the classic dilemma of balancing openness with the demands of mutual respect and care for the other incumbent on an egalitarian discourse ethic). That Habermas does little to refine his model or clarify these dilemmas in *Structural Transformation* itself is beyond dispute: they are precisely the kinds of dilemma that will recur throughout our encounter with Habermas in this book.

2
Discursive Testing:
The Public Sphere and its Critics

This chapter provides a brief overview of some of the critical responses that *Structural Transformation* has provoked. My account will, of necessity, be selective and will focus on those commentaries that I think are useful – even where they are problematic – in helping us to clarify certain important issues *and* in highlighting unresolved dilemmas and tensions within the Habermasian perspective on the public sphere. Given that Habermas's methodology in *Structural Transformation*, which differs markedly from his later work, involves historical excavation in search of a normative model of democracy relevant to the present, many critical commentaries have taken issue with the historiographic credentials of the book. The fact that these historical excavations are carried out in the service of this normative goal means we might be tempted to set such controversies aside as somehow peripheral or pedantic. But, although the Habermasian project as a whole does not rest on historicist foundations, *Structural Transformation* does implore us to learn something from the past and to understand that the values of critical publicity constitute something other than mere abstract morality conjured in a historical vacuum. Moreover, some of the issues raised by historian critics are particularly salient for conceptual discussions of the public sphere. We begin, then, with a brief discussion of historiography which, in its brevity and broad sweep, might not satisfy the historian but which is intended to bring questions of conceptual coherence rather than questions of accuracy to the foreground.

LESSONS FROM HISTORY

Structural Transformation aimed to chart the rise and unfulfilled promises of 'critical publicity'. As with most overtly political history writing, it lays itself open to the charge that the end justified distorted means; that it is simplistic and melodramatic in the contrast it draws between two epochs (liberal and organised capitalism); and that it is overly rigid in its application of two competing categories of publicity ('critical' and 'manipulative') to each respectively. Habermas himself has acknowledged, retrospectively, a disjuncture between his 'fall from grace' narrative and the complexities exposed by more measured historiography: 'my diagnosis of a unilinear development from a politically active public to one withdrawn into a bad privacy, from a "culture-debating to a culture-consuming public," is too simplistic',[1] he concedes.

Such disjuncture, according to Craig Calhoun, is underscored by an imbalanced methodology:

> A central weakness is that *Structural Transformation* does not treat the 'classical' bourgeois public sphere and the postransformation [sic] public sphere of 'organised' capitalism symmetrically. Habermas tends to judge the eighteenth century by Locke and Kant, the nineteenth century by Marx and Mill, and the twentieth century by the typical suburban television viewer. Thus Habermas's account of the twentieth century does not include the sort of intellectual history, the attempt to take leading thinkers seriously and recover the truth from their ideologically distorted writings, that is characteristic of his approach to seventeenth, eighteenth, and nineteenth centuries.[2]

We should bear in mind, though, that Habermas's portrait of the twentieth century in *Structural Transformation* is, rightly or not, premised precisely upon the notion of an alienated post-Enlightenment intelligentsia, now aloof from the morass of popular culture and populist politics. (Tellingly, in fact, Calhoun does not suggest which aspects of twentieth-century intellectual history Habermas *ought* to have drawn more heavily upon.) Moreover, we could equally argue that, in terms of historical analysis, it is precisely the prominent role of those eighteenth- and nineteenth-century intellectual figures which is problematic. For all the interesting historical evidence which Habermas adduces (and to which our synopsis in Chapter 1 could scarcely do justice), he tends ultimately to interpret the eighteenth and nineteenth centuries through the rigidified theoretical frameworks of those great Enlightenment thinkers. It is unsurprising, then, that various critical responses to *Structural Transformation* have drawn on revisionist historiography in order to take aim at the linear sweep of Habermas's narrative.

First, we should take seriously the claim that Habermas's account valorises a particular mode of (bourgeois) 'rational' communication which may, indeed, be discernible from the period he characterises as its heyday, but which may account for only one of various modes of discourse occupying the public sphere. Geof Eley, for example, criticises Habermas for filtering out the myriad agonistic, insurgent, contestatory, and status- or prestige-laden discourses of the liberal–capitalist public sphere in his quest for a relatively purified model of egalitarian, consensual, rational–critical debate.[3] But if Habermas did not give due attention to the plurality of discursive practices and institutions within bourgeois circles, then the way in which he treats non-bourgeois practices and institutions is particularly controversial. This is something which will concern us in the following section (and in subsequent chapters) at a more theoretical level, but the problem of exclusion (particularly the exclusion of women and the working classes) has been flagged repeatedly by historian critics as well as by social and political theorists. Habermas tells us that the public sphere was, from its inception, built on certain exclusionary mechanisms. But Habermas's narrative of exclusion may be flawed. Keith Baker, for example, claims that it was not merely the eighteenth-century bourgeoisie, but also various sites of working-class discourse which contributed to the development of 'critical publicity'.[4] The problem is not that Habermas denies the participation of the working classes (in Jacobin and Chartist guises, for example) in agitating for expanded suffrage, greater press freedom and so on, but rather that he portrays these values as if they were simply derivative of a bourgeois tradition that was the true birthplace of critical publicity.[5] In simultaneously intersecting with and diverging from the dominant bourgeois model,[6] these 'others' are significant for any consideration of the development of 'the' public sphere writ large.[7] For social theorists rather than historians the relative accuracy of competing readings is less important than the lesson of interpretive plurality: we should always remain attentive to the significance of marginal and subaltern political spaces whose existence, but also, more specifically, whose formal and procedural characteristics, fall outside the purview of mainstream narratives of the past, present and future.

A similar problem emerges with the way Habermas portrays the exclusion of women from the political public sphere. Again, the problem lies not so much in Habermas underestimating the forces of exclusion at play within the bourgeois public sphere but in the concept of 'exclusion' itself. As Nancy Fraser puts it, 'the view that women were excluded from the public sphere [is] ideological; it rests on a class- and gender-biased notion of publicity, one which accepts at face value the bourgeois public's claim to be *the* public'.[8] To begin with, Habermas largely (though not entirely) neglects the positive contribution made by women to the advancement of so-called 'bourgeois publicity'. In merely acknowledging the existence of a 'woman-friendly' salon culture, Habermas is somewhat equivocal: the impression could be given (inaccurately, according to feminist historiography) that the 'public sphere' was to all intents an exclusively male preserve to which women were historical latecomers. In fact, whilst women were denied *official* access to the *political* public sphere until well into the twentieth century,[9] feminist historiography has highlighted the role of women in the public sphere from the beginnings of the bourgeois era: as participants in a salon culture *actively marginalised by* (and not born of) a politically ascendant male bourgeoisie, and as participants in publicly active movements and groupings involved, for example, in the promotion of temperance or poverty relief.[10]

Moreover, then, *Structural Transformation* exhibits a tendency, which revisionist historiography cautions against, to portray the exclusion of women from the official public sphere in quasi-natural terms, that is, as if the exclusion of women flowed seamlessly from an ideology of domesticity keeping them in their place. This underplays the history of struggle and the extent to which women's organisations carved out a role for women which, though it may not have aspired to *match* that of men, was nevertheless *public*. They were not simply excluded from the male-dominated public sphere a priori but also actively and coercively, through patriarchal relations of control and economic dependency, and by the hostile environments of the public-sphere institutions themselves: this level of analysis is largely missed by the broad sweeps of *Structural Transformation*. Habermas, we must remember, takes his lead from Marxian ideology critique: he distinguishes between a set of eighteenth-century *ideals* and their imperfect historical manifestation.[11] But the question arises as to whether Habermas's reading of the bourgeois *ideals* is any less problematic than his reading of the institutions and practices that operated under their banner. Was the bourgeois public sphere ideological simply because it was blind to its own contradictions or was it, in fact, more overtly riddled with manifest conflicts, power games and strategic thinking than Habermas allows for? Feminist historiography, at least, makes the latter more plausible.

Structural Transformation also exhibits a tendency not only to overlook the role played by women in the growth of 'critical publicity' but also to overlook the distinctiveness of that role. Like the working-class publics, there were both convergences with and divergences from the dominant male bourgeois model privileged by Habermas.

For example, women's moral-reform groups would often draw on, rather than exclude, putatively 'private' values of domesticity and the care ethic. In other words, women were not only challenging exclusionary forces in order to participate in public life: they were also implicated in a struggle over the very meaning of publicity, and the nature of the boundaries between public and private. As we shall see later, this historical dispute goes to the heart of contemporary issues for the democratic imagination.

What all this points to, then, is a narrative in *Structural Transformation* which sits rather uncomfortably with an array of feminist scholarship. The image of women as relative latecomers is problematic, particularly when combined with a 'fall from grace' narrative in which women are only admitted to the public sphere at a time when its positive attributes have been all but lost under a torrent of massification. Mary Ryan, for example, counters the view that the admission of women to the official public sphere was simply part of that trade-off between democratic expansion and degradation. Women have not only been active in the shaping of modern publicity, but have also engineered certain key qualitative gains in the nature of democracy through, for example, achievements in expanding the political agenda to include sites of power that were once 'private' issues, such as the family and poverty. Women's eventual admission to the 'official' public sphere 'cannot be ironically dismissed with the painful observation that when women finally won the franchise and official access to the public, they found themselves the conquerors of a hollow fortress'.[12] For all the regressive transformations the public sphere may have undergone, it is important to emphasise not only that women played a role in building that fortress, but also that it's distinctly *less* hollow than it would have been had they not battled their way in.

Habermas's emphasis on a very specific social group – the male, property-owning classes – is undoubtedly connected to his emphasis on a novel social formation – modern capitalism – and the new relationships between state and society, politics and economics, which it embodied. It is, then, legitimate to question whether or not Habermas's narrative suffers the burden of those 'historical blinkers' which post-Marxist thought has taught us to associate with reductive, economistic readings of history. Such questions of methodology relate not only to the role played by social groups other than the male bourgeoisie, but also to the role of historical dynamics other than what Marx saw as the self-propelling juggernaut of capitalist accumulation.

David Zaret argues that Habermas fails to account properly for the various historical dynamics which, whilst intimately connected with the capitalist economy, are not reducible to it.[13] The technological development of mass printing, religious developments in the wake of the Reformation, the development of scientific and anthropocentric world-views – in other words, those facets of modernity which, taken together, fed into (and off) the increased confidence and autonomy of the bourgeoisie – do, indeed, lack a suitably prominent position in the narrative of *Structural Transformation*. This isn't the place at which to rehearse that classic duel between Marxian and Weberian paradigms. For now it will suffice to point out that Habermas himself has acknowledged that the economistic bias of this early work was problematic.[14] And as we shall see, Habermas's subsequent attempts to rework the theory of the public sphere decentre the economy and move decisively away from treating 'classes' as economically determined 'macro-subjects'.

EQUALITY AND EMANCIPATION

In writing *Structural Transformation*, Habermas was to a large extent addressing the Left in 1960s West Germany. Peter Hohendahl outlines some of the responses that the book provoked amongst Habermas's target audience.[15] He distinguishes between those Marxist detractors (such as Ulf Milde) who condemned Habermas's 'bourgeois' discourse out of hand and those (such as Oskar Negt and Alexander Kluge) who criticised it as conservative but also saw something important in it that could be rescued. According to Milde, Habermas unforgivably paints the bourgeois public sphere as an embodiment of the principle of freedom; he conceives of bourgeois property relations as apolitical; and he overlooks the role of antagonistic class relations. Hohendahl could swiftly dispense with such a response not because there is no debate to be had about the very possibility (and mystification) of a public sphere free from domination and inequality (and we will return to this question), but because without acknowledging that Habermas's entire thesis rests on the notion of a post-liberal order in which the ideological obfuscations of the bourgeois public sphere are brought out into the open and challenged, such a discussion immediately misfires. Hohendahl speculates on the motives behind such an apparently intentional misreading and suggests a knee-jerk reaction not to the substantive arguments advanced in *Structural*

Transformation so much as to Habermas's methodological challenge
to economistic orthodoxy:

> In the final analysis, Milde's critique is directed against the tendency to
> qualify the orthodox interpretation of the relationship between base and
> superstructure in favor of an approach in which interaction ... is regarded as
> being no less primarily important than work ... The goal of the public sphere
> is intersubjective agreement on values and standards, which can then be used
> to resolve practical questions. What Habermas sees institutionalised in the
> public sphere – individuation, emancipation, extension of communication
> free of domination – appears in [later work] ... under the category of
> 'symbolically mediated interaction.' Since these deviations from orthodoxy
> are voiced already in *Structurwandel der Öffentlichkeit*, the reservations of
> the orthodoxy camp were to be expected.[16]

Two less orthodox critics offered a more considered and less dismissive
critique of *Structural Transformation*. Oskar Negt and Alexander
Kluge[17] took up the category of the public sphere in their own work.
The idea of a democratic public sphere was an important concept
for analysing the possibilities and challenges of progressive social
change that had been lacking in historicist versions of Marxism. The
public sphere was a necessary institutional basis for the formation
of a 'collective will'.[18] But Negt and Kluge disapproved of two key
aspects of Habermas's thesis. First, they criticised his tendency to
take the bourgeois claim that the public sphere could be the site for
clarifying a 'general interest' too much at face value. The unifying
term 'bourgeois' merely conceals the fact that 'what Habermas
had described as an institution turns out to be a loose association
of heterogenous organisations'.[19] (Hohendahl rightly retorts that
Negt and Kluge are unwilling to differentiate between the plurality
of associations and the outwardly consensual orientations which
Habermas ascribes to them and identifies as their unifying principle.
I shall come back to this question of plurality below.)

Second, they condemn Habermas's fixation on the redemptive
powers of discourse. They propose an alternative conception of the
public sphere that is both *proletarian* and which privileges *praxis* over
discourse. Despite the anachronistic language, these tensions in fact
still speak to debates surrounding the public sphere today: actions, for
many, speak louder than words and few use the terms 'talking shop'
and 'the chattering classes' as compliments or badges of honour!
The term 'proletarian', for Negt and Kluge, is not simply about social

status: 'we are starting', they tell us, 'from the assumption that the concept *proletarian* is no less ambiguous than *bourgeois*. Nonetheless, the former does refer to a strategic position that is substantively enmeshed within the history of the emancipation of the working class.'[20] By contrast, 'The bourgeois public sphere is not sufficiently grounded in substantive life-interests.'[21] It discounts productive activity as a legitimate contribution to the public sphere itself. An 'authentic' proletarian public sphere, driven by emancipatory impulses, must be rooted in the autonomous praxis of the working classes: this, unlike Habermas's public sphere, would connect with 'the real experiences of human beings'.[22] For Negt and Kluge, 'praxis' is inclusive: it includes material and cultural production, as well as political action. This inclusive model of participation in the public sphere is a useful corrective to Habermas's rather one-dimensional concern with communication and public-opinion formation in *Structural Transformation*. It reminds us that making an independent film (one of Kluge's own vocations) or setting up a local cooperative in competition with a corporate behemoth can be both an existentially *and* socially 'meaningful' intervention in the public sphere, every bit as much as immersing oneself in political debate. (As we shall see, Habermas's later work is less fixated on 'pure discourse', favouring the ideals of 'communicative action' which allows the *possibility* for switching over to discourse whenever agreements or understandings break down.)

At the same time, Habermas's model remains a useful counterweight to Negt and Kluge's emphasis. In the late 1960s and early 1970s, Habermas was at pains to counter what he saw as the arbitrary 'actionism' of the Leftist student movement in West Germany.[23] It's not hard to see how Negt and Kluge's praxis model flirts with this danger. The term 'proletariat' was, even then, more ambiguous than they cared to admit. The 'working class' was already becoming an incoherent and disparate category, in the context of the rise of 'managerialism', an expanding white collar sector, highly unionised blue collar sectors, diversifying subcultures, migrant workers and so forth. A 'call to praxis', so to speak, devoid of any concern for how to engage people who do not share in a particular vision or who might be affected by someone else's 'praxis' (the groups represented in the independent film, or the employees of the corporate behemoth, say) threatens to remain politically impotent at best and morally suspect at worst. The problem of grassroots campaigners and direct action groups that either won't engage in dialogue with the public at large or *can't* because they are ignored by the media and other public sphere institutions remains a pressing one today. We are not well served by a model of the public sphere that simply substitutes praxis for discourse at its core.

A more recent Marxist reading of *Structural Transformation* was offered by the communications scholar, Nicholas Garnham. On balance, Garnham is more sympathetic to, than critical of, the Habermasian conception of the public sphere. The virtues he ascribes to it are substantial:

> Its first virtue is to focus upon the indissoluble link between the institutions and practices of mass communication and the institutions and practices of democratic politics. Most study of the mass media is simply too media-centric ... The second virtue of Habermas's approach is to focus on the necessary material resource base for any public sphere ... Its third virtue is to escape from the simple dichotomy of free market versus state control that dominates so much thinking about media policy. Habermas ... distinguishes the public sphere from both state and market and can thus pose the question of the threats to democracy ... coming from both the development of an oligopolistic capitalist market and from the development of the modern interventionist welfare state.[24]

Garnham also admires the sharp pertinence of Habermas's thesis to trends, three decades later, of intensified deregulation of the media industries and the now almost taken-for-granted view of information and culture as a 'privately appropriable commodity' rather than a 'public good'. By highlighting the importance of civil society institutions which are independent of both state and market, a text like *Structural Transformation* could, Garnham suggests, inspire the Left to break out from the trap of the free-press model, based on the ideology of a free market place of ideas, which it has often found difficult to critique when the dangers of state interests commandeering the media seem to lurk on the other side.[25] The 'public sphere' concept offers a third term usually lost in the discursive and regulatory switches between state control and marketisation.

Garnham also claims that Habermas's thesis requires some reformulation in order to render it relevant 'to the conditions of large-scale societies in which both social and communicative relations are inevitably mediated through time and space'.[26] Although I explore the question of mediation in Chapter 4, what concerns us here is Garnham's argument that, by comparison with the face-to-face dialogue by which Habermas places much store in *Structural Transformation*, mediated communication presents particular challenges to the principle of universal access, which can only be addressed through redistributive measures. As we saw in Chapter 1, Habermas's analysis does acknowledge the materiality, and not merely the ideology, of the public sphere: unequal patterns of access to time, space, literacy skills and the like underpin unequal opportunities to participate in the public sphere. But it is also true that, under conditions of increased technological mediation, these problems of material inequality are magnified.

Nancy Fraser's reading of *Structural Transformation* addresses the question of whether the Habermasian public sphere can sustain a critique of material inequality whilst engaging with and remaining sufficiently attentive to problems of autonomy, cultural difference and pluralism. Fraser's reading of Habermas has done perhaps more than any other to open up productive lines of inquiry. In the Anglophone community, at least, it is also one of the most frequently cited critiques by those who (unlike Fraser herself) would dismiss the Habermasian understanding of democracy as hopelessly naïve, patriarchal and anachronistic. Given the influential role Fraser's ideas have played in mediating the Habermasian public sphere in recent debates, I will devote some attention to them here.

Aspects of Habermas's theory, Fraser claims, are insufficiently developed to fully withstand the competing impulses of universalism and pluralism but, as a point of departure, Habermas's theory of the public sphere is an 'indispensable resource'.[27] Most importantly, Habermas's focus on a public realm of debate not commandeered by the market or the state provides a counterweight to socialist discourses that conflate state control with 'socialisation' and thus become apologia for bureaucratic, patrician, even authoritarian, statism; and to feminist discourses which conflate the public sphere with the state and/or the official economy, resulting in dubious campaigns for, say, the commodification of housework and childrearing, or increased state censorship of pornography. But the theory of the public sphere sketched by Habermas requires some 'critical interrogation and reconstruction'[28] if it's to provide a productive framework for thinking through contemporary problems. The bourgeois public sphere was based, according to Fraser, on at least three dubious assumptions that lacked sufficient critical scrutiny in *Structural Transformation*. Further scrutiny can, she argues, shed further light on those contemporary problems.

The first assumption was that 'it is possible for interlocutors in a public sphere to bracket status differentials and to deliberate *as if* they were social equals; the assumption, therefore, that societal equality is not a necessary condition for political democracy'.[29] Aside from the actual patterns of unequal access to the bourgeois public sphere, Fraser does not accept that the formal principle of 'participatory parity' was (and is) unproblematic. The bourgeois ideal requires the *formal bracketing* rather than the *elimination* of inequality such that interlocutors of differential status could debate *as if* they were peers.

> But were [social inequalities] really effectively bracketed? The revisionist historiography suggests they were not. Rather, discursive interaction within the bourgeois public sphere was governed by protocols of style and decorum that were themselves correlates and markers of status inequality. These functioned *informally* to marginalise women and members of the plebian classes and to prevent them from participating as peers.[30]

Informal, frequently subtle, modes of domination and control are almost inevitably present in arenas of public deliberation. Already subordinate and under-represented groups tend to be further disadvantaged in their encounters with dominant modes of communication in terms of their capacity and obligation to conform to prevailing conventions of discourse (those pertaining to style, rhetoric, ranking and turn-taking, for example), and their likelihood of being listened to and taken seriously: they often lack the requisite 'cultural capital' (Bourdieu). Feminist research into gender differences in public communication contexts (political meetings, for example) reinforces this observation in a contemporary context. For Fraser, the formal requirement to bracket status differentials can itself lead to mystification, an obfuscation of underlying inequalities, and a bolster to dominant 'default' cultural values.

> Insofar as the bracketing of social inequalities in deliberation means proceeding as if they don't exist when they do, this does not foster participatory parity. On the contrary, such bracketing usually works to the advantage of dominant groups in society and to the disadvantage of subordinates. In most cases it would be more appropriate to *unbracket* inequalities in the sense of explicitly thematising them – a point that accords with the spirit of Habermas's later communicative ethics.[31]

Fraser is certainly correct to note the shift of emphasis in Habermas's later work. However, we should pause before we merrily eject the principle of formally bracketing differences from a progressive model of democracy. Rather than looking at this issue in terms of a binary opposition, it may be more fruitful to consider the value of formally bracketing status inequalities on the one hand and explicitly thematising them on the other as two sides of the same coin, based on the age-old trade-off between responsibilities and rights. Fraser seems, quite laudably, to argue for the 'right' of participants to thematise any perceived inequality which may affect the parity of discussion. On the other hand, the requirement to bracket status differentials could be conceived in terms of the *responsibility* of participants to strive to avoid playing 'power games' within the deliberative arena with the intention of subordinating fellow participants (implicit slurs on someone's background, status, or ethnicity, for example). To simply postulate an ethic of mutual respect does not get us too far in reducing intentional or unintentional, subtle and overt forms of communicative manipulation or bad faith. But ejecting it from our model of democracy would foster a moral vacuum and serve to legitimise domineering techniques of debate and interaction. It's hard to see how this ethic intrinsically contradicts the egalitarian principles Fraser espouses. Rather, it's the failure to marry it to the right to thematise and question asymmetries that is dangerous from a democratic perspective.

For Fraser, however, my corrective would probably miss the main point which is that

> a necessary condition for participatory parity is that systemic social inequalities be eliminated. This does not mean that everyone must have exactly the same income, but it does require the sort of rough equality that is inconsistent with systemically generated relations of dominance and subordination. *Pace* liberalism, then, political democracy requires substantive social equality.[32]

This is a noble ideal but it draws on an undifferentiated notion of equality that limits its theoretical and political value. We cannot realistically avoid the task of differentiating between social inequalities that clearly and significantly impinge upon the fairness and openness of the democratic process and those that do not, though to be sure this is no straightforward exercise and there are no objective, scientific criteria available to us outside of public debate itself. Of course there is a strong connection between one's socio-economic status and one's ability to participate in the democratic process, but the correlation is not simple or linear. At one extreme there are those who cannot access even the most elementary resources for participation such as basic information and access to the media or to education: such stark levels of disenfranchisement exist in most Western democracies and the problem is an extremely urgent one. There are also gender-related issues (including access to childcare and disposable time, for example) which are highly relevant to participatory parity. And, of course, at the top end, corporate power, hereditary wealth and prestige are all clearly factors affecting access to the upper levels of political power. But it does not in any way follow that one citizen always has more power to participate in the public sphere than another simply because of his elevated socio-economic status. To talk of creating minimum thresholds for improving participatory parity based on the provision of universal education, public information services and the like (however this may be complicated by the value judgments involved in applying such a principle in concrete situations – what *kind* of education or information is required?) is a more convincing political or strategic 'first base' than the requirement of even 'rough' socio-economic equality. The point here is *not* to disregard the importance of distributive justice. Rather, I want to claim that the relationship between participatory parity and socio-economic equality is oversimplified in Fraser's critique.

This is not just a theoretical argument. If, as a political project, the 'politics of the public sphere' marks out social equality as prerequisite to a legitimate democracy then the scope for progress is questionable. Fraser glosses over the fact that the relationship between social equality and participatory parity must be conceived as two-way. In this interpretation, participatory status is affected by socio-economic status but, also, socio-economic status is affected by participatory status. Socially disadvantaged groups can find themselves trapped at least partially by their low levels of access to the public sphere. If their voices are not heard then their interests cannot be advanced and the pursuit of greater social equality will be hindered. This is the vicious circle of liberal democracy. There are various possible responses to this vicious circle. One is to rely on the privileged few to speak up on behalf of those lost voices and pursue equality on their behalf. In a world of increasing material comfort for those on the right side of the divide, for whom the underprivileged are largely sequestered from first-hand experience (and subject to narrow stereotyping by the media), this response seems hopelessly naïve at best, and fraught with the ethical dangers of a paternalistic, victim-centred welfarism at worst. A second response is to hold fast to the link between socio-economic equality and participatory parity and therefore fatalistically accept the circle in all its viciousness. A third, however, would be to relativise that link and look towards the virtuous rather than the vicious movement of the circle: the greater the provision of resources for participation in and access to the public sphere, the greater chance disadvantaged groups have of getting their voices heard, of collectively interpreting and articulating their own interests and needs, and of realising greater socio-economic *and* participatory parity. The link between 'life chances' and 'discourse chances', to use a neater vocabulary, is of critical importance to any theory of democracy and it is, as Fraser argues, obscured by classical liberalism and, at best, under-theorised in *Structural Transformation*. The fact that it is also less straightforward than Fraser implies may, in fact, entitle us to a shred more optimism.

A second assumption underpinning the bourgeois public sphere is: 'that the proliferation of a multiplicity of competing publics is necessarily a step away from, rather than toward, greater democracy, and that a single, comprehensive public sphere is always preferable to a nexus of multiple publics'.[33] Fraser's arguments here follow on from her contention (noted above) that 'it is not possible to insulate special discursive arenas from the effects of social inequality'.[34] It follows that, in order to build solidarities, clarify identities, interests and objectives, and to find their 'own voice' independently of the standard modes of talk and the constructions of 'us' (such as the 'national interest' or 'humanity') that covertly serve the interests of the dominant, subordinate groups require their own alternative or 'subaltern' spaces of discursive deliberation.[35] Fraser is quick to point out that not all subaltern publics are democratic and egalitarian in structure. But more importantly, perhaps, she distances her arguments from political and cultural separatism:

> in stratified societies, subaltern publics have a dual character. On the one hand, they function as spaces of withdrawal and regroupment; on the other hand, they also function as bases and training grounds for agitational activities directed towards wider publics. It is precisely in the dialectic between these two functions that their emancipatory potential resides.[36]

Habermas's reading of the bourgeois public sphere also evokes a multiplicity of associations, coffee houses, reading groups and the like which could only be characterised as a public sphere in the singular insofar as the opinions which emerged from them were directed towards each other and towards the same centre of power, namely the state. But Habermas's model is based on a series of associations that were (supposedly) open in principle to all, had potentially fluid networks of membership and cut across special interest groups. Leaving aside the question of historical accuracy, Fraser wants to argue for a model of democracy which emphasises the importance of groupings and publics which are defined by particular sets of interests and memberships. A totalised ethic of inclusivity is not in fact one that sits comfortably with the interests of various subordinated groups. Her arguments do not (and are not intended to) deny the importance of that ethic as a foundation stone for rational public dialogue: if the public sphere is to be conceived as an inclusive auditorium, Fraser's remarks point up the importance of the anterooms around its perimeters, some of which are open and 'inclusive', and some of which are reserved for use by specific groups. Inevitably, the theoretical tools for distinguishing between a 'healthy' pluralism on the one hand, and parochialism and separatism on the other are significantly blunted with this concession, though in any case such reflexive judgments are properly the domain of public discourse *itself*. But the normative *and* sociological value of any theory of the public sphere depends on acknowledging the significant role of subaltern public spheres and particularist public 'sphericules', to use Todd Gitlin's phrase.[37] This insight is all the more important in the context of post-national politics (where in any case the nation state can no longer claim to be a political control *centre* in the sense implied by classical liberal and various leftist models of democracy) and the entropic pressures brought to bear on political processes in the wake of neo-liberal globalisation, multinational corporatism, and the rise of 'postmodern' identity-based, localised, diasporic and tactical political movements (see Chapter 5 for further discussion).

A third assumption is 'that discourse in public spheres should be restricted to deliberation about the common good, and that the appearance of private interests and private issues is always undesirable'.[38] The principle of restricting public discussion to matters of 'public' or general concern causes problems for a theory of democracy:

This is ambiguous between what objectively affects or has an impact on everyone as seen from an outsider's perspective, and what is recognised as a matter of common concern by participants. The idea of a public sphere as an arena of collective self-determination does not sit well with approaches that would appeal to an outsider's perspective to delimit its proper boundaries. Thus it is the second, participant's perspective that is relevant here. Only participants themselves can decide what is and what is not of common concern to them. However, there is no guarantee that all of them will agree.[39]

This observation lends weight to the case for treating the boundaries between the public and the private as both provisional and reflexive. As we have noted, both socialist and feminist politics have reconfigured these boundaries by pushing, respectively, the work sphere and the domestic sphere – hitherto 'private' concerns – onto the public agenda. The boundaries are historically contextual and, for a progressive democratic politics they cannot be fixed a priori but instead remain subject to the push and pull of public deliberation. The virtue of this position is that it avoids the moral vacuum risked by those who reject the very idea of such a boundary on account of historical evidence showing how it has been exploited by patriarchal and capitalist interests using 'privacy' as a cover for manipulative practices: Fraser's corrective reminds us that a politics of the public sphere must, in fact, extend to that liminal zone rather than restricting itself to the comfort zone of a 'natural' public interest. As such, the idea of the public sphere provides resources for dealing with the question of privacy and public interest in a way that avoids the twin pitfalls of ethical relativism and elitism. Ethical relativism is the logical conclusion of a free-market populism (often espoused by popular media) which equates the 'public interest' with whatever the public happen to be 'interested' in, and which is indifferent to questions of prurience and privacy. The elitism often expressed by politicians, on the other hand, looks to opinion leaders and moral guardians to determine the boundaries of public interest and to protect society from its own prurience or from its majoritarian impulse to control, surveil and micro-manage everyday life. The idea of a reflexive public sphere offers us a way into thinking critically about those disciplinary mechanisms (which are in no small part *self*-disciplining mechanisms, as Foucault and his followers have taught us) which target aspects of social life that, in circular fashion, only become publicly consequential (that is, 'moral') by dint of those very surveillance practices. But it avoids pre-assigning aspects of social life to a black box marked either 'private' or 'public': it emphasises the significance of discourses that shed new light on previously hidden arenas of social power and domination, from exploitative employment practices through to domestic or sexual violence.

The fact that so many issues – domestic violence, pornography, smoking in public places, car use, chemical pesticides and the like – provoke not just ethical judgments but also questions about their relevance to the public interest suggests that the terms 'public' and 'private' may be dangerous insofar as they encourage a spatial framework of understanding: we are not simply considering the boundaries between 'areas' of social life but between a vast complex of social phenomena that cut across virtually all domains of society. We might, then, prefer to switch over to the vocabulary of moral philosophy, one that plays a prominent role in Habermas's recent thinking, which distinguishes between particular conceptions of 'ethics' (or 'the good life') and generalisable principles of 'justice' which can accommodate a plurality of ethical positions. But, as we shall see, Habermas argues forcefully that the actual application of principles of justice in the 'public interest' is always already an 'ethical' project that favours a particular 'way of life'. Moreover, the terms 'public' and 'private' continue to pervade cultural and political discourse and the controversies and boundary disputes they give rise to show no signs of waning. We are, then, stuck with a less than perfect vocabulary.[40]

Fraser is right to emphasise the importance of this contestation over the very scope of the public agenda. This includes conflicts over questions of identity, including gender and ethnicity, that may be perceived by some, but not others, as relevant to the distribution of power and status within the public realm itself – something not captured by Habermas's tacit acceptance of the bourgeois conception of the public sphere comprising *private*, ostensibly anonymous persons whose identity and status are matters outside its scope. We need to remember in all this that there are various levels of generality at which public debate can ensue on various topics. There are various ways in which sensitive issues can be publicly debated without necessarily trampling over people's desire for privacy, including fictional media narratives or voluntary (and sometimes anonymous) testimony. Of course, even under such conditions, public 'debate' can still give rise to hysteria and witch-hunts that leave citizens vulnerable to intrusive and oppressive reactions. But the point is that a progressive politics which promotes greater discursive reflexivity on the nature, scope and boundaries of the public agenda need not, *in itself* at least, threaten civil liberties.

But Fraser is not talking simply about *topics* of public interest. She is also raising the question of deliberation oriented towards the establishment of the *common good*:

> This is a view of the public sphere that we would today call civic–republican, as opposed to liberal–individualist. Briefly, the civic–republican model stresses a view of politics as people reasoning together to promote a common good that transcends the sum of individual preferences ... On this view, private interests have no proper place in the political public sphere. At best, they are the prepolitical starting point of deliberation, to be transformed and transcended in the course of debate.[41]

The civic–republican view legitimately corrects the bourgeois model's tendency to view the common good as something given which can be *revealed* through public discussion. The common good is, instead, conceived as something that can potentially be *generated* through dialogue. This is a 'deliberative' model of democracy, one which Habermas revisits in his more recent work, *The Inclusion of the Other* (see Chapter 3). The problem with Habermas's model, however, is that it 'conflates the ideas of deliberation and the common good by assuming that deliberation must be deliberation *about* the common good'.[42] In other words, debate is implicitly trained on the question, 'What will be good for *us*?' This emphasis on the first person plural ('a single, all-encompassing "we"') tends to reinforce the dominance of particular groups and to disadvantage others whose voices have not been well heard in the past and who, therefore, have lacked the power to shape the definition of who 'we' are that now confronts them. Fraser argues, then, that any model of democracy that rules out the articulation of self- or private interests undercuts its own progressive aspirations. 'The postulation of a common good shared by exploiters and exploited may well be a mystification.'[43]

Fraser's emphasis on the need to conceive of the public sphere as not only plural but also allowing for spaces of withdrawal and exclusivity among interest groups rightly addresses the requirement for subordinate groups to reflect on and clarify their identities and interests. We might also add that adversarial encounters and criticism from other interest groups in the public sphere at large can contribute to those processes of reflection and clarification. But we should proceed with caution here. Habermas himself actually develops a model of democracy that can be neatly equated neither with a liberal–individualist nor a civic–republican model. In *Structural Transformation* it was already clear – with the inclusion of plural publics and interest groups as components of an imagined post-bourgeois public sphere – that the ultimate incommensurability of interests in large-scale societies must be given its proper place. It becomes much clearer in Habermas's later work that he uses the notion of the 'common good' in a very particular way. Habermas is actually concerned with the *orientation* rather than the *outcome* of public discourse. The model works only on the premise (which cannot always be assumed) that participants engage in public discourse with a degree of good faith and countenance at least the possibility that they may be persuaded to modify or even set aside the views they started out with: this is where Habermas's deliberative model departs both from models of democracy that reduce the public sphere to nothing more than an arena for the clash of views or the thrashing out of grudging compromises, *and* from the hubris of Enlightenment humanism.

The public sphere in the Habermasian sense is an arena in which the *possibility* of understanding and agreement is tested.[44] It's not the achievement of a consensus that is the test of 'rational–critical' debate. Rather, it's the extent to which the procedures allow for the *possibility* of an uncoerced consensus to be *tested*. The pursuit of greater parity within the public sphere and the impulse to shed light on the interests that underscore competing positions is precisely the basis on which Habermas imagines a public sphere that can chip away at the mystifications of false consensus. For Habermas, the public sphere itself, rather than critical theory, must become the very locus of ideology critique. This emphasis on reflexivity is often lost on Habermas's critics. Bruno Latour, for example, caricatures the Habermasian public sphere as a 'club' where 'men of good will assemble with cigars ... and leave their gods on hooks in the cloakroom'.[45] But in fact it's not so far removed from Latour's own sense of a 'constructivist cosmopolitics' wherein a shared cosmos is precisely the energising potential and not the precondition of globalised discourses – a bottom-up cosmopolitanism, in other words, as opposed to a 'fundamentalist' cosmopolitanism which graciously invites 'Others' to join a Western club of 'unencumbered' and 'rational' humanity.[46]

RATIONALITY AND EMBODIMENT

Habermas's rationalism is, indeed, a target for many critical commentaries. Most operate at the level of formal philosophy. Here I will focus on just two critiques that engage rather more directly with the politics of the public sphere. Both link the question of rationality with that of bourgeois impulse towards disembodiment. The privileged place of the printed word and of the principle of indifference towards identity both underscore this linking of rationality and disembodiment. Habermas, though, has been reluctant to problematise this link.

John Durham Peters questions Habermas's disdain for the 'representative publicity' of both pre- and post-bourgeois formations and the way in which he pathologises politics functioning as a spectacle as opposed to a participatory forum.[47] *Öffentlichkeit* in *Structural Transformation* connotes the openness associated with rational discussion of matters of state rather than the shadowy secrecy concealed behind either the showy displays of status associated with feudalism or the public relations-fest of advanced capitalism.

> Representation, in both the political and aesthetic senses of that term, has a curious place in Habermas's theory of communication. First, in *STPS* Habermas is suspicious of representative government. *STPS*'s model of democracy ... is participatory: democracy is the identity of the citizens and the government ... Ideals of participatory democracy often go together with a distrust of aesthetic representation; the two attitudes have an elective affinity. Habermas prizes conversation, reading and plain speech as worthy forms of discourse for a democratic culture and is frankly hostile to theatre, courtly forms, ceremony, the visual, and to rhetoric more generally.[48]

Peters believes Habermas's preference for a particular form of political culture betrays a Protestant asceticism. '"Communication" for Habermas is a resolutely sober affair ... He slights the Dionysian side of language, its dangers and irrationalities and its creative bursts.'[49]

But the point of Peters' critique is not simply that the Habermasian public sphere is culturally skewed. Habermas's particular preference serves, in fact, to undermine his own ideal of inclusive democracy. In the first instance, it conjures up a rather empty, formal 'utopia' of rational discussion that leaves critical theory ill equipped to address the motivational deficits of contemporary democracies.[50] (We will revisit this problem in subsequent chapters.) But, more importantly, the ideal of unrestrained dialogue evokes an aspiration for co-presence among citizens that may have fit the ancient Greek *agora* but not the conditions of large-scale, modern societies. As Peters points out, Habermas's more recent work discards the fallacy of co-presence, that is, the identity of citizens and government. (Our reading of *Structural Transformation* suggests, in fact, that this was always the case.) But in that case, asks Peters, why does Habermas continue to hold fast to a rationalist conception of communication and to condemn the aesthetic spectacle of representative publicity as a threat to democracy? If, in complex, large-scale societies, we cannot all be equal participants at all times in the political process then political communication will inevitably involve spectatorship. To condemn outright all modes of representative publicity is to condemn the very processes that make possible membership of and involvement in a political community. Aestheticisation is also enfranchisement.[51]

At the same time, Peters does nothing to distinguish the necessary embodiment of representative structures from an untrammelled aestheticisation of politics. There is, indeed, a necessary connection between representative structures and aesthetic communication. Once we discard the fallacy of communicative transparency in a complex world, we see that mediated and condensed symbols of trust, status and aura will play their part in the democratic process. But these considerations are always relative. After all, it would be difficult to argue that *any* piece of political communication – technologically mediated or otherwise – does not carry with it an aesthetic or expressive dimension, whether or not that is the intention of the speaker. The sincerity or aura of the speaker and the imaginative appeal of the visions they evoke, are invariably subject to a certain aesthetic judgment by citizens. Habermas's later theory of 'communicative action' rests precisely upon the notion that ordinary speech encompasses expressive, normative and cognitive dimensions simultaneously.

Representative structures demand a certain communicative 'short-circuiting' which implicates the mass media (see Chapter 4) and the partial displacement of cognitive utterances by expressive or emotive symbols. But this stops short of accepting the inevitability of a predominantly aestheticised politics. The mere fact of representative political structures and mass mediation does not, of itself, condemn the public sphere to a politics of style without substance. Habermas himself may be suspicious of communication beyond the written and spoken word and Peters is correct to question that. I shall argue later that this logocentrism is neither productive in an intensively mediated society nor necessary for a critical perspective on the public sphere. But one of the virtues of the Habermasian model is that it emphasises the role of criticism within the public sphere. It invites us to imagine how cognitive, normative *and* expressive utterances might be subjected to 'discursive testing' more readily than they are in the present. This means interrogating the accuracy and rightness of claims made by power holders and by citizens themselves. But it could equally mean debating the sincerity of an aesthetic or expressive gesture: 'What does that smile, that slick turn of phrase or that sartorial finesse actually conceal?', for example. Of course, we cannot hope and shouldn't want to fully 'rationalise' the public sphere and purge it of all aesthetic and expressive signs. In this sense the logocentric and scientistic tenor of the phrase 'discursive testing' may be counterproductive. But a more open public sphere is one which allows for more people to participate in the production of all kinds of utterance, for dominant rhetorical and aesthetic strategies to be met with alternative rhetorical and aesthetic strategies as well as with wordy debate, and for citizens faced with the aesthetic spectacles of the powerful to find creative ways of 'answering back'. In that sense, we must look to democracy itself, rather than the sobriety of discourse, to 'rationalise' power.

In his critique, Peters defends the ideas of Richard Sennett against critical remarks made by Habermas.

> What Sennett laments as a 'fall' in public life – the replacement of more or less flamboyant forms of personal display in dress, speech and demeanor by private, 'intimate' forms of sober self-expression – is for Habermas a step towards a more democratic mode of civil society.[52]

I suggest that Habermas should indeed take Sennett's ideas more seriously, but for a slightly different reason from that given by Peters. In his discussion of political charisma Sennett argues that late-twentieth-century politics became dominated by a form of personality politics based not on the flamboyance and aura of political leaders but on their banal humanity – their 'controlled spontaneity'[53] – training eyes on trust and integrity as a stand-in for substantive political debate. Rather than dismissing this 'secular charisma' as an irrational form of politics, he instead invites us to consider both its rational causes and its irrational consequences.

Secular charisma is rational; it is a rational way to think about politics in a culture ruled by belief in the immediate, the immanent, the empirical, and rejecting as hypothetical, mystical or 'premodern' belief in that which cannot be directly experienced. You can directly feel a politician's sentiments; you cannot directly feel the future consequences of his policies.[54]

The suggestion is that perhaps contemporary politics, tabloid sex and corruption scandals notwithstanding, *is* all too sober and all too rational such that the 'real issues' (which are complex) are obscured by personalities and reputations and only rear their heads too late: once the consequences of policies can be felt directly. The rational ends of democracy depend paradoxically on our willingness (or our ability) to embrace something less than purely rational. What's required are leaps of imagination, and 'political fantasies' through which we can disengage ourselves from the immediacy of personality-based politics and address those issues that exceed the banal immediacy of contemporary political culture. Here is a worthy challenge to Habermas's sober rationalism and I shall be revisiting the notion of political imagination (as 'counterfactual thought') in the final chapter. Habermas and Sennett both share a critique of personality-dominated politics. What Sennett alludes to (and what Habermas would no doubt find uncomfortable) is ostensibly a more 'visionary' mode of politics that focuses the mind on the 'what ifs' of policies and decisions.

Peters writes that 'beyond all symbolic politics, for Habermas, lurks the king's body, which must not be resurrected'.[55] This may be a plausible reading of *Structural Transformation*, less so of Habermas's more recent work in which, for example, he engages with questions of identity-formation and cultural renewal. But regardless of this, Peters gives the misleading impression that, if we take Habermas's ideal of rational political communication seriously, we must be indiscriminate in our condemnation of 'symbolic politics', and that our only alternative is to be indiscriminate in our *embrace* of aestheticisation. Would we then find it difficult to distinguish between the media gossip around politicians' sexual indiscretions and the images of violence or suffering in one of the world's many conflict zones? Both function as aesthetically loaded symbols that stand in for cognitive insight: often, such representations are mind-blowingly superficial or downright misleading. And yet some symbols are more relevant than others to the formation of democratic mechanisms of control: some energise public discussion and further scrutiny of public policies and institutional practices, whilst others undeniably obscure and deaden public debate in favour of spectacular infotainment. It is true that aesthetic symbols can mediate large-scale 'imagined communities' in Benedict Anderson's sense.[56] But it is also true that they can feed irrational hatreds and exclusions. It may also be true that his personal memories of Nazism predisposed Habermas to an excessive reaction against aestheticised politics: after all, Nazism remains a 'sobering' reminder of the dangers of excessively aestheticised politics! Peters' wisdom that symbolic politics is 'more than Nuremburg rallies'[57] invites us not simply to embrace a more 'catholic conception of (mass) communication, appreciative of its gloriously raucous as well as soberly informative qualities',[58] but, rather, to investigate ways in which we might untangle its progressive and destructive threads.

Michael Warner's critique of Habermas emphasises the role of desire in the public sphere, something which seems extremely marginal to Habermas's narrative. Central to Warner's argument is the relationship between the public sphere and the body. The 'universal reason' of the bourgeois public sphere was exercised according to the ability to detach from the particularities of the self:

> In the bourgeois public sphere, which was brought into being by publication ..., a principle of negativity was axiomatic: the validity of what you say in public bears a negative relation to your person. What you say will carry force not because of who you are but despite who you are. Implicit in this principle is a utopian universality that would allow people to transcend the given realities of their bodies and their status. But the rhetorical strategy of personal abstraction is both the utopian moment of the public sphere and a major source of domination. For the ability to abstract oneself in public discussion has always been an unequally available resource.[59]

Bodily identity is most readily disregarded when a citizen belongs to the dominant or 'default' group, which was white and male in the case of the bourgeois public sphere. At one level, this is a development of the theme introduced by Fraser (see the previous section): only when personal attributes perceived to impact on the fairness of the public sphere itself may be explicitly articulated and debated can the power relations of the bourgeois model come under challenge. But the process of 'refeudalisation' described by Habermas has indeed, via the visual media, placed the body at the centre of the public sphere:

In earlier varieties of the public sphere, it was important that images of the body *not* figure importantly in public discourse. The anonymity of the discourse was a way of certifying the citizen's disinterested concern for the public good. But now public body images are everywhere on display, in virtually all media contexts. Where printed discourse formerly relied on a rhetoric of abstract disembodiment, visual media ... now display bodies for a range of purposes: admiration, identification, appropriation, scandal and so forth. To be public in the West means to have an iconicity.[60]

Warner questions the wisdom of reading this 'mass publicity' and iconicity as a pathological deviation from the rationalist ideal of self-abstraction. He goes further than Fraser, then, by arguing that such an ideal not only worked against 'minoritised subjects' but also against 'privileged subjects' as it 'abstracted from the very body features that gave them the privilege of that abstraction'.[61] Self-abstraction is a denial, a form of 'bad faith'. At the same time, however, a 'longing' to 'abstract [oneself] into the privilege of public disembodiment',[62] a longing to rise above our bodily characteristics and limitations, remains heavily ingrained in our culture (consider, for example, the excitement around 'identity play' stimulated by Internet chat rooms, or the explosion of 'vanity publishing' through web logs and home pages). There is a resultant tension between self-realisation and self-denial. This, says Warner, is where consumer capitalism, the mediator of contemporary iconicity, plays its part:

> Part of the bad faith of the *res publica* of letters was that it required a denial of the bodies that gave access to it. The public sphere is still oriented enough to its liberal logic that its citizens long to abstract themselves into the privilege of public disembodiment. And when that fails, they can turn to another kind of longing, which ... is not so much to cancel out their bodies as to trade in for a better model. The mass public sphere tries to minimise the difference between the two, surrounding citizens with trademarks through which they can trade marks, offering both positivity and self-abstraction.[63]

Consumer capitalism provides a kaleidoscopic array of images and brands (attached to commodities and icons) which, through positive or negative appropriation 'make available an endlessly differentiable subject'.[64] Positivity is articulated through strategies for the definition of the self; self-abstraction is addressed not through the anonymity of print but through the anonymous (market) entry into the public exchange of symbols. Against Habermas, then, Warner suggests that 'the public sphere is not simply corrupted by its articulation with consumption. If anything, consumption sustains a counterpublicity that cuts against the self-contradictions of the bourgeois public sphere.'[65] This in turn helps to explain the prevalence of the politics of identity and difference in recent decades.[66]

Habermas himself finds it difficult to recognise the relevance of Warner's narrative to a theory of democracy.[67] But there *are* some pertinent issues at stake here, even if we do not concede such a foundational role to desire and self-contradiction as Warner's psychoanalytic view of the subject embraces. The productive aspect of treating consumerism as a site of 'counterpublicity' lies not in substituting a Frankfurt School view of the consumer as hapless victim for a celebratory postmodern view of the consumer as a 'semiotic guerilla' (Eco[68]). Instead, it reminds us to take seriously the seductions of a culture that hails us as consumers rather than citizens. Consumerism may be seductive not simply because, following Adorno, our spirits have been dulled by the routines and rhythms of modern life. It may also be a site that, in the absence of better alternatives, offers some kind of a framework for working through issues of self-identity. Consumerism, as we know, is not a domain of social life that is somehow separate from the political public sphere: the logic of consumerism has in large part pervaded the political public sphere itself. If, in *Structural Transformation*, Habermas seemed to take at face value the bourgeois principle of bracketing questions of identity, his later work (Chapter 3) highlights the role public life can play in the processes of identity formation. But his emphasis here is on questions of cultural and group *belonging*. He does not have much to say about the public dimensions of individual self-identity which, as postmodern discourse has suggested, may be best understood as an ongoing project of *differentiation* within networks of signification. The desire to simultaneously identify *and* differentiate, which seems to be the piston of contemporary consumer culture, is not taken especially seriously by Habermas. But if we were to take this seriously, and to acknowledge that it implicates the political public sphere as well as the shopping mall, what would we have to take account of?

We might recognise not only that the public sphere is populated with *bodies* as well as words, thoughts and ideas, but also that it is shot through with tensions and contradictions that make the pseudonymous writer of letters to the editor, the poster of Nelson Mandela, the rubber George W. Bush mask worn by the protestor, and the music played at a political rally, all of a piece. The Internet has become something of a microcosm for these tensions and contradictions (Chapter 4). It affords anonymity and disembodiment but also possibilities for reconfigured embodiment (the carefully crafted self of the personal home page, for example, or the 'identity play' of the chat room or virtual community). The point is that our model of the public sphere should account for, rather than simply pathologise *tout court*, the role of bodies, icons and desire. At the same time, it must continue to question the scope that exists for both criticism and diversity, and the uneven levels of access to these sites of (dis/re)embodiment enjoyed by different citizens.

3
Reconfigurations: The Public Sphere Since *Structural Transformation*

In this chapter we trace some of the key developments in Habermas's thinking on the public sphere since *Structural Transformation*. The political public sphere has not received the same degree of explicit attention in his subsequent writings but, despite the broad territory over which Habermasian critical theory has ranged, the concept has remained implicitly and stubbornly central throughout.

In *Structural Transformation*, as we saw, Habermas combined discussion of the substantive history of the public sphere with contemporaneous intellectual discourses on the concepts of publicity and public opinion. During the late 1960s, in a series of important essays (collected in English under the title *Toward a Rational Society*),[1] Habermas focused on the task of developing a conceptual apparatus with which the social sciences could approach problems of democracy. But the essays were strongly wedded to their particular historical context. They were written in the shadow of vociferous student protest and talk of a 'new sensibility' which stood opposed to the stifling consensus politics and productivist ideologies of post-war Germany. These essays remain insightful today because they help us understand the trajectory of Habermas's thinking on the public sphere. But they also provide some food for thought in the context of contemporary debates. We will begin here, then, before considering some of Habermas's later conceptual manoeuvres.

SCIENTISM AND POLITICS

A central problematic for Habermas at this time was captured in the title of one of his essays: 'The Scientisation of Politics and Public Opinion'. The target of his critique was the consolidation of a 'scientistic' model of politics, a model which envisaged a set of relationships between 'experts', political leaders and the citizenry very differently from either the bourgeois model elucidated in *Structural Transformation* or Habermas's own radicalised post-liberal model. Scientism was, according to Habermas, heavily infused into the political culture and institutions of the post-war democracies (particularly the Federal Republic) although it was the intellectual affirmation of the scientistic model – a then-prevalent positivism – which provided the main target for his critique.

Positivism, of course, has roots stretching back through the Enlightenment to figures such as Comte and Hume. But the recent memories of acts carried out in the name of National Socialist (and Soviet) 'science' gave added impetus to the struggle to purge political values from science: to remove all traces of normativity would be to ensure the unhampered production of 'valid' knowledge, and to liberate science from co-option and distortion by ideological interests. In political science, specifically, the project to separate the 'is' and the 'ought' had been advanced previously by Weber and Schumpeter and was now (in the late 1960s) 'unquestioned by modern political sociology'.[2] The fundamental premise of a positivist social science was that: 'from theoretical knowledge we can at best, given specific goals, derive rules for instrumental action. Practical knowledge, on the contrary, is a matter of rules of communicative action and these standards cannot be grounded in a scientifically binding manner.'[3] To that extent, the proper role of political science was to describe, model and predict measurable phenomena and the causal relationships between them, (the relationship between a political campaign and its likely efficacy, for example), and not to evaluate or judge the moral implications of goals pursued within the political realm. The outcome would be an 'apolitical' political science. Science could furnish special interest groups, such as parties, with knowledge, so long as the divorce between theory and politics remained sacrosanct.

Habermas considered two sub-models of political scientism, both of which have implications not only for the internal functioning of political science but for conceptions of the political realm itself. Both raised particular claims about the relationships between experts (including political scientists themselves), politicians and the citizenry. The 'decisionistic' and the 'technocratic' models, discussed by Habermas, are best conceived not as mutually exclusive black boxes but as poles on a continuum. The *decisionistic* model occupied the more intellectually modest end of the continuum with Weber figuring as the key influence.[4] Here, science imagined itself to have a critical but self-limiting role within the political process: it could provide instrumental knowledge and assessments of political *means* but it could not apply scientific rationality to the process of selecting between competing political *ends*. It called for a careful division of labour between 'politicians' who carry forward the values and goals of society, on the one hand, and scientific 'experts' on the other. Decisionism fatalistically accepted an irrational core at the heart of political decision making. As for the citizenry at large, the decisionistic model tended to conceive its role in plebiscitary terms as the periodic acclamation and legitimation of the politicians. It would be counterproductive and inefficient to have a citizenry engaged in protracted deliberation over ultimately non-rationalisable values.[5] Whilst a particular society may have an ethical preference for democracy, the only 'rational' basis for public input was, ultimately, to avert the entropic consequences of a legitimation deficit.

By comparison, the *technocratic* model sought to enlarge the scope of scientific rationality. It didn't exclude outright the possibility of rationalising political power.[6] The feasibility and the consequences of political goals themselves could be rationally assessed. Taken to its logical conclusion, the technocratic model evoked a society in which values (ends) are derived *from* technology (means). A cybernetic system of feedback control made critical reflection on social values redundant because their validity could be read off from their contribution to the smooth reproduction of the 'system' itself, in the context of its changing 'environment'.

The technocratic model demanded a radical reappraisal of the relationship between experts and politicians. In the decisionistic model the expert was conceived as dependent on the political actor. The expert would be called upon to assess mechanisms for achieving a prescribed range of goals. In the technocratic model the relationship between political actor and expert was reversed. The techniques developed by experts would shape the goals of the political actor. Though few today would openly endorse the hard-nosed version of technocracy described here, this intellectually 'passé' model still looms large in contemporary debates about political culture: the term 'pragmatism' is routinely invoked either affirmatively to champion the passing of ideology and dogma in politics, or pejoratively to decry the rise of the technocrat and the career politician for whom values seem to be invoked only opportunistically.[7]

Obviously, the Machiavellian motif of the politician as, first and foremost, a tactician or strategist is no more a distinctively late modern phenomenon than is the charge of naïve idealism levelled at those who demand that politicians act first and foremost as moral agents. However, the technocratic model signalled at least one distinctively modern aspect: political 'techniques' (including public relations as well as public administration) would become a rapidly developing and expanding area of 'scientific' inquiry and knowledge production – a major growth industry of the twentieth century, in fact.

One important ambiguity in the technocratic model was not problematised by Habermas. This is probably because it's an ambiguity that also pervaded Habermas's own thinking at this stage. The problem is whether the technocratic model rests on the assumption of a successful (or potentially successful) diffusion of a 'technocratic consciousness' among the citizenry. It's not clear if the public must necessarily endorse expertocracy, or whether a fatalistic orientation or, say, the distractions and seductions of leisure and consumption, might suffice. The technocratic model can, in theory, live without the assumption of a powerful technocratic ideology by conceiving the public realm as an environmental variable to which the political system must always be ready to adapt. In contemporary political culture there is, in fact, an ongoing tension between the opportunistic deployment of moral and ethical rhetoric ('populism'), examples of carefully moderated procedural visibility (the televising of parliamentary debate, for example), and esoteric language games that signify the impenetrability of the political 'system'.

For Habermas, the technocratic world-view pervading political culture was dangerous. He sought to challenge the integrity of both a technocratic model premised on the fact or possibility of hyper-rationalised political discourse, and a decisionistic model premised upon the fact or possibility of a clear division between evaluative and cognitive discourses. This challenge was part of a wider and, at the time, controversial attack on positivism.[8] A recurrent theme in that dispute was the positivistic ideal of isolating discourses of facts and norms from one another, whilst this 'purified' scientific paradigm refused to acknowledge its own internal values, namely a partisan commitment to the principles of 'Reason', enlightenment, truth and 'progress' and a crusade against dogma and myth. But, according to Habermas, the technocratic and decisionistic models of political science each have their own specific flaws (and even some advantages). Habermas himself concurs with the principle that values cannot be deduced from facts.[9] But this doesn't mean that values can somehow be purged as in the technocratic imagination, or institutionally separated as decisionism suggests. The idea that political science can be insulated from specific value positions is untenable.

Technocrats erroneously imagine that the political ends they pursue are intrinsic rather than the product of human decisions.

But the smooth reproduction of a system through adaptation to changing environmental variables (or, indeed, the historically necessary replacement of a moribund system, as in Marxist variants of the technocratic imagination), is not a goal. It's an abstract idea (based on the human impulse to refashion social systems in the image of natural systems) which frames competing interpretations of 'reproduction' and 'environment', and concrete policy proposals.[10] Decisionism models, on the other hand, acknowledged an irreducibly contingent core at the heart of political decision-making processes whilst upholding the myth of a value-free scientific domain, as if experts could proceed only in the service of truth and did not have to make choices and selections according to exterior motives – ethical impulses, political views, competition for research funding and so forth. The decisionistic model laid itself open to the charge of political relativism. The technocratic model at least had the virtue of inviting a less fatalistic attitude, upholding scientific rigour as the last line of defence. Habermas himself adheres to a model of democracy premised on rational standards of communication but, as we shall see, his vision of a self-limiting *procedural* rationalism differs greatly from that of the technocratic imagination.

The technocratic ideal falls short on at least three counts. First, it fails to reflect properly on the key values (including principles of 'unconstrained discussion', 'uncompelled consensus' and the horizontal ethics of peer review)[11] which implicitly underpin the scientific community and serve as evaluative criteria for 'good science'. Second, it fails to recognise that these criteria may also be productively applied to normative discourses: within the scientific community itself, questions and statements of 'ought' (relating to the comparative merits of various research proposals in terms of ethics or community benefit, for example) are as prevalent as those relating to the communication of facts and results. The principles of dialogic exchange and unconstrained discussion are, as we saw in *Structural Transformation*, those that Habermas believes must be applied to *all* types of normative discourse. Third, however, Habermas claims that these scientific standards, contrary to the positivistic perception, do in fact reflect a particular and historically located set of goals – those of 'truth', 'demystification' and 'progress'. To that extent, then, if Habermas himself is to avoid falling into the relativism and irrationalism for which he criticises decisionism, he must articulate why these very European-sounding virtues are more than *just* values, more than just impulse reactions driven by a distaste for political relativism or by fear of the technocratic 'nightmare' of a 'totally administered society'. In these early essays, however, this level of critical reflection is missing.

Habermas's critique of scientism could, of course, be rescued from the charge of arbitrariness by reading it in context of a particular Zeitgeist. The student movement rejected the culture of positivism pervading the universities and the technocratic ideology underpinning the post-war political arena: in the FDR in particular, the new generation rejected the idea of sweeping the horrors of the past under the carpet of a new objectivism. But Habermas was not simply an intellectual mouthpiece for the new generation; he was also one of its critics, especially when he perceived the activities and beliefs of the counter-culture to be degenerating into an anti-science irrationalism. In its critical stance towards scientism, Habermas saw in the student movement a potential to reframe and renew the Enlightenment project by bringing science, morality and aesthetics into a more balanced encounter with each other. Instead, it seemed to adopt rebellion for rebellion's sake, short-circuiting rational debate on the means and the ends of the protest: Habermas accused it of degenerating into 'arbitrary actionism'.[12]

The argument between Habermas and the leaders of the student movement was famously escalated by Habermas's accusation of 'Leftist fascism' – an ill-judged turn of phrase, by Habermas's own admission,[13] but one which captured his horror at the sight of a movement challenging the positivistic divorce between theory and practice only to disavow the former and therefore maintain the divorce under a different guise. The implications were, at worst, anti-democratic and violent. Habermas could not accept the rejection of instrumental reason per se and the reaction against technology. The student movement and, what's more, his own Frankfurt School predecessors,[14] were in Habermas's eyes, wont to confuse the ubiquity of instrumental reason with its mere operation. Outright antipathy towards pragmatic discourses dealing with political strategy, technological means and so on, was to damage rather than advance the cause of breaking the spell that scientism had cast on the political sphere. In the student movement, rational discourse on the means of achieving its goals was in short supply. But Habermas points beyond this: it is also possible and necessary, he argues, to rationalise the *process* by which the goals themselves are developed. Here, in the heat of political controversy, Habermas was articulating a core goal that would henceforth shape his entire intellectual project: namely, to develop a model of '*procedural* rationality' by which we could judge the legitimacy of procedures for argumentation, agreements and compromises.

Habermas, then, wanted to carve out a third space between positivism and the 'voluntarism' he saw pervading the student movement. He proposed that we aspire to a vision of a democratically structured society that would embody 'the dialectic of enlightened will and self-conscious potential'.[15] We should respect the integrity of scientific and evaluative discourses by acknowledging both their analytical autonomy *and* their practical interdependence: the language of science, of technology, of means, always entails normative considerations, just as the language of values, goals and ends, misfires when it's unhinged from pragmatic considerations. Acknowledging and institutionalising this interdependence and autonomy would, for Habermas, be the real mark of enlightenment. But where the 'discourse of potential' lends itself to a division of labour between experts and lay actors (which has somehow to be mediated), only citizens themselves have privileged access to the needs, desires and aspirations that constitute the other moment in that dialectic.

But, still, it's another thing altogether to demonstrate why, in particular, a universal, democratic and egalitarian institutionalisation of 'will' makes for a more 'rational' (rather than merely ethically preferable) organisation of society. If the ideals of unforced consensus, peer scrutiny and unconstrained discourse make for 'good science' (and some may question even this), why do these standards necessarily make for 'good values' and 'good morals', over and above other historical standards such as tradition, religion, birthright and the like. These essays cannot tell us why. But they provide a compelling critique of the contradictions and distorted self-understandings of political scientism – and therefore still have something to say about the contradictions of political culture today; and they may offer us some insight into today's protest movements which, like the anti-globalisation movement, are still implicated in that tension between 'actionism' and the need for debate about alternative directions for society.

SYSTEM, LIFEWORLD AND COMMUNICATIVE ACTION

If the aims of *Structural Transformation* were ambitious, they were nothing compared to those of Habermas's *The Theory of Communicative Action*. Here Habermas set out to achieve no less than a systematic theory of modernity and a reconstruction of the foundations of social science. Habermas is an eclectic but honest scholar who acknowledges his debts to the great figures of social theory whilst setting out to reformulate some of their central ideas. *The Theory of Communicative Action* is an immense and frustratingly dry piece of scholarship.

But the narrative of modernity and rationalisation developed in *The Theory of Communicative Action* does resonate with the narrative of the public sphere developed in *Structural Transformation*: in both, the tale is one of missed opportunity, of suppressed emancipatory potential and of modest fragments of optimism scattered across the wasteland. Moreover, the concept of the public sphere is critically important in *The Theory of Communicative Action*, even though it is not the main focus of analysis. Rather than trying to follow every twist and turn of this two-volume work, our purposes here are best served by an initial statement of its main theses. In the first instance, Habermas argues that in order to comprehend processes of social development and reproduction, we must engage 'society' at two levels, at the level of the 'lifeworld' and at the level of the 'system'. At the level of the 'lifeworld' we aim to make sense of social processes as the outcome of social actors' intentions and value orientations. At the same time, the consequences of social action routinely exceed actors' intentions: at the level of the 'system' we aim to comprehend the manner in which social actions intermesh above the will and/or consciousness of social actors. Habermasian sociology, in other words, aims to combine 'systems-theoretic' approaches favoured by deterministic Marxism and functionalism, on the one hand, with 'action-theoretic' approaches characteristic of Weberian sociology, hermeneutics and phenomenology, on the other.

The development of modern societies can be grasped as a process of progressive rationalisation. But this insight depends on a particular conception of rationality. 'Purposive-rational' (or 'strategic') action is made synonymous with rationality itself in so much social theory, including Marxism, Weberian approaches, the writings of the Frankfurt School, and those of Michel Foucault. But this is a one-sided account of rationality. Habermas's three-dimensional model not only considers the possibility of 'rationalising' expressive, aesthetic and 'dramaturgical' actions in the strictly limited or procedural sense we have already discussed at the end of Chapter 1;[16] it also argues for treating both strategic and dramaturgical models of action as derivative of and subordinate to a third model that he calls 'communicative action'.

Habermas's concept of communicative action is a product of the 'linguistic turn' in social theory. Adorno as well as Foucault and the 'post-structuralists' had claimed that the Enlightenment 'philosophy of consciousness' – which assumes that 'the solitary subject confronts objects and becomes reflective only by turning itself into an object'[17] – had run out of steam. Whilst Adorno lamented the alienating impulse to objectify the inner and outer worlds, the 'post-structuralists' showed how that impulse was necessarily thwarted by the webs of discourse and textuality through which it always already operates. At the same time, Habermas argues, both camps in their different ways (Adorno's *Kulturpessimismus* versus the ironic, self-referentialism of the post-structuralists) bow to this negativity: neither really exorcises the philosophy of the subject, they just carry out endless post-mortems.[18] This motivates Habermas to try to find a linguistic turn that, unlike the one taken by the post-structuralists, doesn't lead down a philosophical cul-de-sac. He turned to linguistics and speech act theory in order to displace the emphasis on the subject with a focus on questions of *intersubjective understanding*. What 'speech act theory' enables us to do, in Habermas's view, is to reveal universally unavoidable 'presuppositions' behind everyday language use ('universal pragmatics').[19] If we are prepared to give up on the task of elucidating universal aspects of subjectivity, we can instead focus on the more modest task of understanding the conditions under which reasonable, workable communication takes place. Such a task does not rest on a fallacy of perfect communication but on the basis that we use communication to try to reach acceptable (that is, legitimate) understandings, agreements and compromises with each other.

According to the theory of universal pragmatics, whenever we communicate (through language or through action), we unavoidably 'take up relations' to a number of 'domains of reality: "the" world of external nature; "our" world of society; "my" world of internal nature'; and to the medium of language itself.[20] The distinction between 'society' and 'nature' is not one of institutions versus trees and birds. 'Nature' refers to the domain of facticity that comes into existence whenever we take up an 'objectivating' attitude to something (institutions and even other individuals routinely become 'second nature'). 'Society' is constituted whenever we take up a first person plural orientation towards something. Whenever we communicate, *assuming we mean to be understood*, we explicitly or implicitly raise 'validity claims' relating to those domains: correctness in our assertions about 'external nature', legitimacy in our moral view of society (which includes the legitimacy of the utterance itself – that it is our place to say or do this), sincerity in expressing our inner selves, and comprehensibility in relation to our use of language. Every utterance, in this view, has a performative dimension or 'illocutionary force' even where this is hidden beneath the surface.[21] Even a purely descriptive statement *offers* the hearer the possibility of new understanding of reality.

If a hearer is to be *persuaded* (rather than simply coerced) to accept the state of affairs offered by the speaker, the validity claims raised by the speaker have be redeemed or *be seen as potentially redeemable*. Different types of validity claim require different modes of redemption. 'We understand a speech act when we know what makes it acceptable.'[22] What makes propositional truth claims acceptable is the availability of 'grounds' or supporting evidence. Of course, disagreement on the adequacy of grounds or evidence is commonplace in everyday communication. But if we turn this principle on its head, we recognise that a lack of any such grounds makes propositional claims immediately unacceptable. Likewise, we judge the validity of normative claims against the availability of reasons[23] and we start from the premise that the absence of any reasons invalidates the claim. Sincerity claims are judged somewhat differently, not through discourse itself but in the degree of consistency between the speaker's expressions and their subsequent actions.[24]

In most everyday communication, of course, most validity claims are not 'discursively tested'. The normal flow of communication depends in large part upon the assumption that the speaker could, if called upon, redeem her validity claims:

> a speaker owes the binding ... force of his illocutionary act not to the validity of what is said but to the *coordinating effect of the warranty* that he offers: namely to redeem, if necessary, the validity claim raised with his speech act.[25]

In large part, everyday interaction proceeds on the basis of 'good faith' between social actors. But tokens of good faith are not condemned to circulate arbitrarily or on a purely irrational basis of blind trust but, rather, according to the existent possibility that the speaker could, at any time, be called upon to redeem his validity claims. In other words, our assumptions of good faith are all the more precarious where that potential is blocked.

This conception of universal pragmatics lies at the heart of Habermas's model of 'communicative action'. Communicative action encompasses two types of action which, in practice, combine in varying measures. At one extreme 'discourse' explicitly thematises validity claims and subjects them to discursive testing. At the other extreme, 'consensual action' operates against the backdrop of intersubjectively recognised validity claims[26] and on the basis that it could, at any time, be suspended in favour of discourse whenever the consensus comes into question.

Communication, of course, often resembles something other than 'communicative action'. It's often used strategically to engineer consent by *blocking* discursive testing (shouting and sarcasm are just two perennially popular tactics); and it's often deployed with the aim of generating ambiguity (as in many forms of aesthetic communication, for example).[27] So why does Habermas privilege this consensual ideal of speech and action? For Habermas, these other pervasive modes of interaction are not separate from but *derivative* of communicative action itself.

The goal of persuasion implicitly gestures towards egalitarian relations, according to Habermas: 'The illocutionary force of a speech act consists in its capacity to move a hearer to act under the premise that the engagement signalled by the speaker is seriously meant.'[28] A 'speech-act-immanent obligation' (to provide grounds, to justify and/or to demonstrate sincerity if called upon) empowers the hearer (in a limited sense) just as the illocutionary force of the speech act itself empowers the speaker. The 'ideal speech situation' consists in equality between interlocutors and the unhindered scope for each to question and defend validity claims.

Habermas's 'ideal speech situation' has always provoked controversy. We can only begin to take it seriously, of course, if we acknowledge its status as a counterfactual. It is something that Habermas believes is *anticipated* in communication – an unspoken aspirational norm, rather than a concrete possibility. Precise equality between fellow interlocutors would be as difficult to imagine as it would be to measure:[29] in reality participants will occupy differential levels of authority to act as 'final arbiter' when the inevitable constraints of time are faced; some participants, more than others, will command high levels of implicit trust in the validity claims they raise because of their status or reputation – they will evoke less discursive testing; and the discrete boundedness of communicative encounters implied by the terms 'ideal speech situation' or 'reciprocity' is shattered by mediated communication which scatters participants across space and time. In the case of mass mediated communication, the 'ideal speech situation' is a weak metaphor indeed for democratic aspirations of greater diversity or more egalitarian forms of access: literal reciprocity *between* 'speakers' and 'hearers' is largely alien to mass mediated communication.[30]

And yet, for Habermas, all instances of speech gesture towards this counterfactual 'ideal situation'. Every speech act *implies the possibility* of 'uncoerced consensus'.[31] He arrives at this conclusion by conceiving of 'derivative' modes of discourse in terms of 'blockages' in the testability of validity claims – blockages which, through history, have been progressively challenged by humans societies. In this conception, 'communicative action' spans all three 'domains of reality' ('the', 'our' and 'my' worlds) and the corresponding validity claims (truth, rightness, sincerity), whereas the three models of action which loom large in the sociological literature (strategic, norm-guided, and dramaturgical action) are 'one-sided' in their privileging of specific reality domains and validity claims. Only communicative action privileges the discursive testing of all three types of claim and the interplay of first, second and third person perspectives.

> The one-sidedness of the first three concepts of language can be seen in the fact that the corresponding types of communication singled out by them *prove to be limit cases of communicative action*: first, the indirect communication of those who have only the realisation of their own ends in view; second, the consensual action of those who simply actualise an already existing normative agreement; and third, presentation of self in relation to an audience. In each case only one function of language is thematised: the release of perlocutionary effects, the establishment of interpersonal relations, and the expression of subjective experiences. By contrast, the communicative model of action ... takes all the functions of language equally into consideration.[32]

For Habermas, then, the model of communicative action functions as a framework for analysing the shortcomings and blockages of extant practices, discourses and institutions.

In addition to this synchronic argument for treating communicative action as a kind of meta-model, Habermas wants to ground its privileged status in a historical narrative of the 'unfolding' of communicative potentials in modern society which invokes that distinction between system and lifeworld. The 'lifeworld' is, for Habermas, 'the horizon within which communicative actions are "always already" moving'.[33] Social actors approach every situation from a particular horizon of understanding: 'Every new situation appears in a lifeworld composed of a cultural stock of knowledge that is "always already" familiar.'[34] The conservatism of the lifeworld is disturbed only to the extent that new encounters (with the social, objective or subjective worlds) render *'limited segments'* of the lifeworld problematic, explicit and open to reflection and critique.[35]

Despite being tied to this horizon of understanding, and despite the idealist bent of the philosophical traditions from which Habermas develops the concept (hermeneutics and phenomenology), Habermas alerts us to the *material* basis of the lifeworld: the lifeworld develops not only in a symbolic environment but also materially 'through the medium of purposive activity with which sociated individuals intervene in the world to realise their aims'.[36] The lifeworld, then, does not simply float in the ether of ideas but also encompasses meaningful activities and practices. In that case, Habermas's argument that the public sphere has migrated to the 'system' and needs to be brought back into the meaningful horizon of the lifeworld seems quite at home with the open conception of praxis- as well as discourse-laden public spheres that we discussed in Chapter 2.

The term 'system' is used by Habermas to capture the 'unintended consequences' of social action, that is, to account for the 'coordination' of action in complex societies through non-discursive 'steering media'. Here,

> Media such as money or power can largely spare us the costs of dissensus because they uncouple the coordination of action from consensus formation in language and neutralise it against the alternatives of achieved versus failed agreement ... Media steered interactions can be spatially and temporally interconnected in increasingly complex webs, without it being necessary for anyone to survey and stand accountable for these communicative networks ... If responsibility means that one can orient one's actions to criticisable validity claims, then action coordination that has been detached from communicatively achieved consensus no longer requires responsible participants ... The other side is that relieving interaction from yes/no positions on criticisable validity claims ... also enhances degrees of freedom of action oriented to success.[37]

For Habermas, system and lifeworld have become uncoupled in modernity with ambivalent consequences:

In societies with a low degree of differentiation, systemic interconnections are tightly interwoven with mechanisms of social integration; in modern societies they are consolidated and objectified into norm-free structures. Members behave toward formally organised action systems, steered via processes of exchange and power, as toward a block of quasi-natural reality; within these media-steered subsystems society congeals into a second nature. Actors have always been able to sheer off from an orientation to mutual understanding, adopt a strategic attitude, and objectify normative contexts into something in the objective world, but in modern societies, economic and bureaucratic spheres emerge in which social relations are regulated only via money and power. Norm-conformative attitudes and identity-forming social memberships are neither necessary nor possible in these spheres; they are made peripheral instead.[38]

On the one hand, the lifeworld is progressively 'rationalised' to the extent that 'problematic' segments are increasingly subjected to critical scrutiny rather than remaining fixed by traditional world-views and ideologies. On the other hand, the 'de-linguistified' steering media of money and administrative power lessen the burden on citizens inhabiting increasingly diverse lifeworlds to achieve consensus in everyday interaction. As such, they constitute an essential bulwark against the continuous threats of conflict and dissensus.

But modernity's rationalisation has its dark side in the guise of a 'colonisation of the lifeworld'. Modernity progressively uncouples communicative action from 'concrete and traditional normative behaviour patterns' placing ever greater emphasis on language as the medium of social integration: 'in this respect, value generalisation is a necessary condition for releasing the rationality potential immanent in communicative action'.[39] But rather than simply compelling us to rely on discourse to find ways of living together in an increasingly pluralistic and individualised society, the uncoupling of system and lifeworld also increases the scope for switching away altogether from communicative action and increasing opportunistic, instrumental action orientations mediated via power and money. The increasing autonomy afforded to power and money as steering media in modern social formations opens up more space for the free play of systemic interaction.

The problem, for Habermas, is not the relative autonomy of money and power per se, which keep conflict at bay and afford social actors the space to pursue their own goals in complex differentiated societies. The problem is the pervasiveness of these non-discursive media, which 'connect up interactions in space and time into more and more complex networks that no one has to comprehend or be responsible for'.[40] Money and administrative logic increasingly pervade those aspects of social life which are most valued as sites of 'meaning' in which social actors develop understandings and interpretations of the subjective, social and objective worlds. The commodification of culture; the interventions of expert systems into everyday life signalled by the culture of welfarism; and, importantly, the co-option of institutions of the public sphere by financial and strategic interests: these processes are now conceived by Habermas in terms of a 'colonisation of the lifeworld' by the system.

The role of law in modern societies takes on a particular significance in the colonisation of the lifeworld thesis. For the most part, the non-discursive media of money and administrative power are, *in the last analysis*, institutionalised in law:

> law now has the position of a metainstitution; it serves as a kind of insurance against breakdown ... The political order as a whole is constituted as a legal order, but it is laid like a shell around a society whose core domains are by no means legally organised throughout.[41]

In order to afford social actors the space to pursue their own goals within differentiated societies, law in modernity has become differentiated from morality. The medium of law prescribes moral *boundaries* for social actors but remains indifferent to the moral world-views and motives of actors remaining within those boundaries. Law necessarily affords social actors the opportunity to adopt opportunistic and unreflective orientations towards law. The danger, for Habermas, is that opportunistic orientations become all-pervasive. Where citizens are not engaged in public spheres critically reflecting on the norms of a society's legal framework, law itself congeals into an arcane 'second nature', fatalistically externalised by social actors. Habermas terms this phenomenon 'juridification'.

The increasing mutual autonomy of legal, moral, aesthetic and scientific discourses is, in fact, a function of the *rationalisation* of the lifeworld, rather than its colonisation. But rather than just advancing under conditions of mutual autonomy, Habermas argues that these spheres of discourse have become pathologically insulated from one another, fragmented into expert cultures. Discourses of morality, aesthetics and science all take on the appearance of 'second nature' systems mediated through power (e.g. law), money (e.g. the commodification of culture) or a combination of the two (e.g. science and technology). This bleak picture of modernity draws inspiration from Weber who

> saw the noncoercive, unifying power of collectively shared convictions disappearing along with religion and metaphysics ... A reason restricted to the cognitive–instrumental dimension was placed at the service of a merely subjective self-assertion. It is in this sense that Weber spoke of a polytheism of impersonal forces, an antagonism of ultimate orders of value, a competition of irreconcilable gods and demons.[42]

Society can only reconcile these competing demons under a blanket of systematisation. For Habermas this results in 'a technicising of the lifeworld that robs actors of the meaning of their own actions'.[43]

But Weber's iron cage may not be locked on all sides. Alternatives exist not in new universal ideologies but in practices and institutions that challenge the omnipotence of 'system imperatives' by carving out spaces of articulation and discursive deliberation. For Habermas, many recent 'social movements', including environmental and feminist movements, decentre questions of the distribution of wealth and power and bring conflicts around 'the grammar of forms of life' into the foreground.[44] Challenging the expansive scope of instrumental rationality may take conservative or fundamentalist forms which valorise traditional ways of life; or they may take discursive, critically reflexive forms that gesture towards cooperative methods of debate, decision making and action.[45] In normative terms, what Habermas's theory of communicative action gestures towards is the (re)invigoration of public spheres rooted in the lifeworld, and a dynamic interplay of cognitive, normative and expressive discourses.[46] The point is not to break up the expert cultures that have grown up around science, morality and law, and aesthetics, nor to underestimate the advances their mutual independence has brought about. Rather, the point is to imagine mechanisms for re-embedding these expert cultures into the lifeworld and to find ways of reconnecting them to each other as well as to the public.

THE POLITICS OF THE OTHER

In Habermas's more recent writings, we can identify some key shifts in emphasis. The first of these is an increased concern with the problem of law and its relation to morality. In particular, he focuses on issues of constitutionalism, the idea of a post-national cosmopolitan law, and the question of human rights. On the surface, at least, this drift seems to represent a rather undesirable turn away from the problems of the 'everyday' lifeworld in favour of a focus on large-scale institutional structures. Habermas's critical theory seems to become rather aloof from the grassroots concerns of the social and political movements to which he appealed in his earlier work. I want to try and rescue the notion of a bottom-up, as opposed to top-down, project of communicative democratisation from this later work (though as I shall argue, the term 'bottom-up' is a reductive shorthand). Paradoxically, however, Habermas's recent work, despite this 'macro-juridical' drift, does in fact engage with issues of cultural difference, cultural power and the cultural dimensions of citizenship and democracy, much more explicitly and in greater depth than his earlier writings. In one sense there is a greater 'localism' as well as a greater 'globalism' at play now. We can think of this as an 'ethico-cultural' shift because, in emphasising the importance of *particular* cultural life forms for any understanding of contemporary citizenship and democracy, it brings ethical, and not just moral, dimensions to the surface.

The ethico-cultural shift in Habermas's later writings impacts not only on the interpretation of contemporary political problems but on the status of critical theory itself. Habermas has provided compelling arguments against the nihilistic and relativistic implications of the post-structuralist turn in critical theory.[47] At the heart of these arguments – though there is not space to rehearse them at length here – is Habermas's accusation of 'performative contradiction', namely the tendency within post-structuralist thinking to deploy rational argument to negate or at least undercut the very idea of reason; and to mount the grandest of narratives in a crusade *against* grand narratives. But Habermas has struggled to establish universalist foundations for his own theory of communicative rationality without lapsing into metaphysical thought, abandoning an early project to elucidate a so-called 'quasi-transcendental' emancipatory human interest,[48] turning instead to the 'universal pragmatics' of everyday communication. Whilst he has never given up on the idea that the theory of communicative action is more than *just* a contingent and ethnocentric preference for a particular way of life, he has certainly conceded that it makes sense only in the context of the development of a culturally located 'ethos' which favours communicative over 'costlier' (namely violent or atomistic and opportunistic) approaches to the problems of citizens living together.[49] Habermas now speaks of 'discourse ethics', a model which aspires towards more open, egalitarian, frank but respectful dialogue between citizens with differing interests and backgrounds who want to find better ways of living together.

> The four most important features [of discourse ethics] are: (i) that nobody who could make a relevant contribution may be excluded; (ii) that all participants are granted an equal opportunity to make contributions; (iii) that the participants must mean what they say; and (iv) that communication must be freed from external and internal coercion.[50]

Although discourse ethics aspires to orient participants towards the 'moral point of view' (to address the question of what is right or best for all concerned and not just what is good for me or for my 'community'), it is in itself not a universal morality. When we remember that what we are talking about is not simply a set of abstract ideals, but the institutionalisation of discourse in real, historically specific public spheres, we realise that discourse ethics must be located somewhere in time and space; it must be 'peopled' by real live, embodied citizens who inhabit particular lifeworlds; it will accrue codes, conventions and characteristics that can never be culturally neutral. Spheres of communicative action are always already 'ethically patterned' and culturally located: political cultures will (or must be allowed to) develop in different ways across time and space.[51] At the same time, Habermas refuses to concede that the fundamental pragmatics of discourse or 'argumentation' are culturally peculiar (a claim which would in any case substitute one form of ethnocentrism for another): 'we may assume that the practice of deliberation and justification we call "argumentation" is to be found in all cultures and societies (if not in institutionalised form, then at least as informal practice) and that there is no functionally equivalent alternative to this mode of problem solving'.[52]

On the one hand, then, Habermas upholds a humanistic faith in the communicative impulses of the world's citizens. On the other hand, this is not in itself sufficient to guarantee the spread of communicative rationality in the real world: Habermas has been forced to adopt the ultimately rather modest claim that the basic presuppositions of argumentation '*may* provide an *opportunity*, given the predicament posed by the pluralism of worldviews',[53] and we may only '*hope* that processes of socialisation and political forms of life meet them halfway'.[54] Why should we want to take up an orientation towards the moral point of view? 'An assessment of morality as a whole is itself not a moral judgment but an ethical one ... Life in a moral void would not be worth living.'[55] Our orientation towards morality cannot, then, be uncoupled from questions of identity and who 'we' are *as a species*. Habermas's 'species ethics' represents a minimalist and provisional form of humanism, then. Nonetheless, it does cling stubbornly to a residual humanism – something widely declared moribund in today's intellectual landscape.

The cultural specificity of discourse ethics applies in the sphere of law as well. In *The Theory of Communicative Actions*, Habermas concluded by posing the problem of a divorce between morality and law as the latter takes on the systemic features of 'juridification'. In the two subsequent collections of essays *Between Facts and Norms*[56] and *The Inclusion of the Other*, this problem became his starting point. In complex modern societies law can never be synonymous with morality because legal discourses 'also involve empirical, pragmatic and ethical aspects, as well as issues concerned with the fair balance of interests open to compromise'.[57] Laws 'are too concrete to be legitimated solely through their compatibility with moral principles'.[58] But rather than thinking in terms of either a divorce or conflation between morality and law, Habermas suggests that we approach the problem in a dialectical fashion. Law should be conceived in terms of a dialectic between *private autonomy* and *public autonomy*. Private autonomy delimits 'a protective cover for the individual's ethical freedom to pursue his own existential life-project'.[59] Public autonomy, on the other hand, grants citizens the rights and wherewithal[60] to contribute discursively to the authorship of the legal norms which delimit that private autonomy. This does not mean that in any large-scale community the distinction between legislators and the addressees of law could be extinguished, of course, but the politics of the public sphere aspires to improve the mediation of the two spheres.[61]

Neither public autonomy (privileged in republican thought) nor private autonomy (privileged in liberal thought) must be given primacy. Rather, the two 'reciprocally presuppose one another'[62] and 'it is left to the democratic process continually to define and redefine the precarious boundaries between the private and the public so as to secure equal freedoms for all citizens in the form of both private and public autonomy'.[63] This leads Habermas to make a particular intervention into the debates surrounding human rights and civil liberties:

> Human rights may be justifiable as *moral* rights; yet as soon as we conceive them as elements of *positive* law, it is obvious that they cannot be paternalistically imposed on a sovereign legislator. The addressees of law would not be able to understand themselves as its authors if the legislator were to discover human rights as pregiven moral facts that merely need to be enacted as positive law. At the same time, this legislator ... should not be able to adopt anything that violates human rights. For solving this dilemma it now turns out to be an advantage that we have characterised law as a unique kind of medium that is distinguished from morality by its formal properties.[64]

On one level, then, we can simply read into this the rather laudable aim of trying to rescue a notion of human rights (*not in itself* a uniquely Western concern, as some would have it) from the paternalistic, occidentally skewed and dogmatic fashion in which it tends to be invoked by so many 'global' institutions (a kind of 'human rights fundamentalism'). A reflexive, cosmopolitan institutionalisation of human rights would (a) engage properly with the fact that human rights do not operate in a cultural vacuum and (b) aspire to include not only the full range of states but also a representative range of citizens residing within them (who often do not share in the majority world-view of a particular state territory) in an ongoing deliberative dialogue about the meaning and application of human rights in different contexts. Similarly, within states, the paternalistic and normalising functions of a constitution (for example, the cherished 'right' to an education which may, in fact, be culturally skewed towards specific communities or function as an expert system severed from in-depth public understanding and deliberation) can only be ameliorated by the growth of vibrant, pluralistic and reflexive public spheres of debate. But in each case, such deliberation *presupposes* much of the (concrete) normativity to which it is expected to contribute: a right to freedom of association, for example; or supranational bodies which institutionalise actionable rights to mount a legal challenge against one's own state; or the right to an education that equips us to participate as citizens.

This begins to sound worryingly like an ethics which, rather like the Kantian imperative we visited in Chapter 1, is left to pull itself up by its own bootstraps. On the one hand, the democratic impulse leads us to imagine increasingly abstract constitutional norms that aspire to include the hypothetical *anyone*; on the other hand, we cannot conceive of those norms as *too* abstract, as to do so would be to miss the ethical patterning that inevitably shapes their realisation in practice (thus occluding questions of power), *and* it would mean we aspired to norms so inclusive that they seemed to belong to and therefore to motivate *no one*. To conceive of constitutional norms (including human rights) as purely moral constructs is both misleading and dangerous in that sense. Somewhere, there is a missing term. For Habermas – in recent work, at least – the missing term is 'political culture', a democratic *Sittlichkeit*, a dose of Hegelian tincture to soothe the Kantian pains of abstraction. I want to outline the basic trajectory of this move and summarise some of its virtues. But I also want to argue for a more urgent missing term – *people*, to put it most glibly – and to argue for bringing Habermasian critical theory a little further back down to earth.

To begin with, we should restate a very fundamental premise of Habermasian critical theory: communicative action doesn't function simply to *reveal* consensus or possibilities for compromise or even the ultimate incommensurability of interests. It does not simply explicate preformed private interests. Rather, its function is conceived as productive and processual: it is *deliberative*. Discourse brings new possibilities for self-understanding, reflection and adjustment: this trajectory may be towards greater dissensus, rather than consensus, of course (our world-views develop in negative as well as positive relativity to the 'Others' we encounter). But discourse is neither a billiard table nor a melting pot but something more akin to the cultural air we breathe. Whilst Habermas has not found it necessary (let alone desirable) to announce the death of the subject under the impact of the linguistic turn, he accepts the view that we can only know ourselves and others through the lens of discourse, both actual and imagined. Deliberative models of democracy, such as Habermas's, do not foreground the hopes that public communication can initiate a 'meeting of minds' in the sense John Durham Peters has imputed to the Western 'dream of communication'.[65] Instead, they foreground hopes of establishing territory *through* public discourse which, in all our differences and disagreements, we can occupy together in order at least to continue arguing reasonably with each other. To be sure, there are different visions of deliberative democracy which place differing levels of burden on the democratic process. But towards the minimalist or proceduralist end of the spectrum, where recent Habermasian critical theory is located, it is not the dream of communion that is at play but the hopes for a continual reworking or carving out of sufficient fragments of a shared way of life or common purpose to keep us deliberating, arguing *and reaching compromises* about the ways in which we wish to live better together.

In fact, the Habermasian framework is not *quite* so far removed from Laclau and Mouffe's influential model of 'agonistic pluralism',[66] which emphasises the ongoing struggles between competing cultural, political and ethical discourses, as is widely assumed. This, despite Laclau continuing to paint Habermas as the naïve universalist who pathologises dissensus.[67] What in fact distinguishes Habermas's approach is *not* outright antipathy towards argumentation and particularism but, rather, a stubborn insistence that, if we aspire to see *argumentation* gain ascendancy over *coercion* in the public realm (even where that very distinction remains a topic of debate), then it's necessary to engage in the tricky business of imagining democratic norms which, though they could never operate in a cultural vacuum, could reasonably motivate a diverse citizenry to *favour* argumentation over 'costlier' alternatives.

This is the procedural bias in Habermas's thinking: he emphasises the task of developing constitutional structures that reflexively aspire towards greater and greater inclusivity, autonomy from the majoritarian or elitist traditions of established political cultures, and the nourishment of a sufficiently concrete and motivating *ethos* of democratic citizenship in pluralistic societies. Habermas develops a term for this ethos which is sufficient to make the hairs on the back of the neck stand up for anyone aspiring towards a progressive politics, even those of a republican hue: the term he coins is 'constitutional patriotism'. It's necessary first of all to identify some of the unfortunate but ultimately misleading connotations of this concept before we consider its real merits and pitfalls. The gendered etymology of the term 'patriotism' (from the Latin *patriota*, meaning *fellow* countryman, and the Greek *patris*, meaning *father*land) combines unhappily with the contemporary associations of chauvinism and the ethno-nationalist politics of the post-cold war world. But these are precisely the connotations that Habermas is challenging us to think beyond. *Constitutional* patriotism is one of those intriguing oxymorons – rather like the idea of post-traditional traditions – that invite us to think beyond established binaries. How can a sense of psychological investment or of 'feeling at home' in a democratic polity be uncoupled (which is not to say magically insulated) from localised narratives of what it means to live a good life? And to what extent can we get beyond seeing the nation state functioning as the natural host for such patriotisms?

But more unsettling is the sense that precisely this trope is already the currency of a noxious globalism that has come to prominence since (but certainly did not begin with) the catastrophic events of September 2001. The clash of two fundamentalisms pits a politics of religion against a religion of politics. The US President and his British assistant assert precisely the patriotism of a 'way of doing things' (constitutional democracy and the norms of capitalist globalisation) which is supposedly colour blind, inclusive, international and ethnically neutral, against their ideological opponents. Rather than sidestepping Habermas's formulation as a potentially dangerous apologia for a smug and aggressive 'end of ideology' globalism, a more productive response would be to see how it could be used to orient a thoroughgoing critique of a mythologised constitutional patriotism, something even more urgent now than at the time Habermas was formulating his ideas.

But Habermas does not intend the term to serve only as ideology critique in the negative sense. He's seeking a positive basis upon which *new* bonds of solidarity might emerge between people who wish to retain diverse cultural identities. The term 'constitutional patriotism', however linguistically vexed, can be productive in engaging with contemporary challenges of cultural politics and political culture. The first merit is precisely that it pushes us into thinking beyond the nation state. In *The Inclusion of the Other*, Habermas traces something of the prehistory and modern emergence of the nation state, acknowledging an ongoing tension, stretching back through the Middle Ages and the Roman Empire, between civic and ethnic narratives of political community.[68] The achievement of the modern nation state was to facilitate societal integration and solidarity between strangers at a time when world-views were fracturing, societies were becoming more complex, and people were becoming more mobile.

But nation states have emerged as deeply ambivalent entities that have seen rights of membership paternalistically conferred on citizens through the construction of various shades of *Volksnation* narrative that project an artificial sense of homogeneity and common descent:

> only a national consciousness, crystallised around the notion of a common ancestry, language and history, only the 'consciousness' of belonging to 'the

same' people, makes subjects into citizens of a single political community – into members who can feel responsible *for one another* ... The counterexample of the United States does demonstrate that the nation-state can assume and maintain a republican form even without the support of such a culturally homogeneous population. However, in this case, a civil religion rooted in the majority culture took the place of nationalism.[69]

Today, as is well known, the nation state is under immense strain from the increasingly global flows of capital, media, people, hazards and technologies. Under such conditions, the politics of ethnonationalism have been in defensive ascendency. Rather than condemn the nation state as wholly redundant or regressive, though, Habermas reminds us of its ambivalence:

Though the nation-state is today running up against its limits, we can still learn from its example. In its heyday, the nation-state founded a domain of political communication that made it possible to absorb the advances in abstraction of societal modernization and to re-embed a population uprooted from traditional forms of life in an extended and rationalised lifeworld through the cultivation of national consciousness.[70]

This may look like a strategically glib reading of history. But the point is that Habermas wants to rescue the republican kernel that at least idealistically underscored the emergence of the nation state, namely a political culture that is capable of including and drawing upon a large, complex citzenry in all its diversity. The point is to think this through at institutional levels other than that of the nation state, including regions, supranational bodies such as the European Union, and cosmopolitan arrangements that allow for citizens to begin to 'belong' to the hitherto phantasmagoric global political communities in whose name institutions from the UN to Amnesty International frequently purport to speak. It means challenging the cultural patriotism of the popular media; it means imagining ways in which the European legislature (rather than executive) could be rendered more powerful *and* accountable simultaneously; it means imagining a cosmopolitan order in which the membership, representation and accountability of supranational institutions could be mediated through filters other than the nation state, including non-governmental institutions that are themselves made more accountable than at present; it means much more besides. If all this sounds ridiculously idealistic or simplistic, we should remember that

Habermas has really done no more than to try to point our heads in what for him is the right direction: his intention is not to elide the scale and complexity of the tasks facing the democratic project in the twenty-first century.

A second and related virtue of the constitutional patriotism perspective is the scope it offers for thinking beyond the troubled discourse of multiculturalism. It certainly does not answer the challenges of cultural pluralism, immigration,[71] or indigenous minorities per se. But it does usefully gesture towards the ideals of building political cultures which, rather than treating cultural diversity simply as a challenge to be accommodated or kept in check, treats it instead as the very lifeblood of a democratic ethos. Habermas's antipathy towards the discourse of multiculturalism (by which he actually means a rather brittle and narrow, yet institutionally powerful version of it), is motivated firstly by a critique of essentialism which treats citizens' identities as fixed and reducible to just a few markers (religion, mother tongue, ancestry etc.) and which remains awkwardly silent on the question of citizens who develop a critical stance towards aspects of their 'own' heritage. As Cronin and de Greiff put it in their introduction to the English translation of *The Inclusion of the Other*:

> Because respect for the integrity of individuals ... requires respect for the contexts in which they form and sustain their identities, Habermas is led to defend policies that supporters of multiculturalism also endorse, such as multicultural education, governmental support for the cultural activities of minority groups, and the like.[72]

Habermas accepts the notion of collective rights but, unlike communitarians such as Charles Taylor, he does *not* accept either their primacy over individual rights (they must be 'co-original') *or* the notion of a collective right to cultural 'survival':

> [T]he individual remains the bearer of 'rights to cultural membership', in Will Kymlica's phrase. But as the dialectic of legal and factual equality plays itself out, it gives rise to extensive guarantees of status, rights to self-administration, infrastructural benefits, subsidies, and so on. In arguing for such guarantees, endangered indigenous cultures can advance special moral reasons arising from the history of a country that has been appropriated by the majority culture ... [But] in the last analysis, the protection of forms of life and traditions in which identities are formed is supposed to foster the

recognition of their members; it does not represent a kind of preservation of species by administrative means ... Cultural heritages and the forms of life articulated within them normally reproduce themselves by convincing those whose personality structures they shape, that is, by motivating them to appropriate and continue the traditions productively ... For to guarantee survival would be to rob members of the freedom to say yes or no.[73]

Habermas argues for a 'politics of recognition' in the public sphere that addresses the shortcomings of both liberal individualism and the well-intentioned multiculturalist politics of equality by emphasising a more inclusive and reflexive 'dialectic of legal and factual equality' embedded in a political culture that 'belongs' equally to those affected by it:

Moral universalism must not take into account the aspect of equality ... *at the expense of* the aspect of individuality ... The equal respect for everyone else demanded by a moral universalism sensitive to difference thus takes the form of a *nonleveling* and *nonappropriating* inclusion of the other *in his otherness*.[74]

The 'politics of recognition' is an ethic of rebuilding public cultures of citizenship scaffolded by institutional structures and legal guarantees that enable all citizens to feel included and, should they wish, to become involved in the authorship of those institutions and laws. Its undoubted merit is the way it orients our thinking beyond various dominant discourses of public culture in today's liberal democracies. These include: a politics of polite tolerance which grants 'difference' a space of its own – some special seats in parliament, some cultural funding or some guaranteed media exposure, for example – but little positive role in the constitution of the 'mainstream'; the benevolent but paternalistic invitation to people from 'other cultures' (usually an essentialist or reductive conception) to be admitted into 'our' prefabricated community of citizens; and the related, unreflective claim that 'our' political culture is indifferent to cultural background, that 'anyone' can potentially feel at home in it, and that to open it up to new cultural influences – *new ways of doing things* – would be to negate this neutrality. For Habermas, it's important that a political culture of 'equal respect' should not be conditional on the value that the dominant culture places upon other cultures: 'the right of equal respect has nothing to do with the presumed excellence of his or her culture of origin'.[75] The development of a 'constitutional patriotism', then, suggests the need to build a political culture that's oriented towards *unconditional* respect for the 'Others' with whom our fate is unavoidably linked; and it also suggests that such a political culture must open itself up to new and diverse cultural influences – to invoke Latour again, it must *not* make the disingenuous demand that citizens leave their cultural coats on cloakroom hooks before they enter the public sphere. The intrinsic tensions of this public ethic (to respect others *regardless* of their cultural identity without *disregarding* or demanding that they disregard that cultural identity) may simply invite us to throw it into the 'too hard' basket. But it may also vouch for its relevance to a complex problem: we would do well to discard simpler remedies.

But there is a troubling bias in Habermas's recent theorising around the public sphere that places limitations on its relevance and value. The emphasis is on (re)connecting citizens with the political culture of an official republican polity. I want to suggest that whilst this is undoubtedly an important and urgent area of analysis, it puts the *conceptual* if not the *historical* cart before the horse. Also in urgent need of interrogation is the role and scope of communicative action in the array of 'micro-publics' that populate contemporary society, and which, for the most part, entertain rather finite or piecemeal aspirations, but which often prove more effective in drawing citizens out into the public arena than the grandiose concerns of the official polity and its satellite fora, such as mass political parties or large scale non-governmental organisations. I think Habermas ends up by underestimating the extent of disconnection between most citizens in Western liberal democracies and the official political and legislative processes. General allusions to 'social movements' notwithstanding, Habermas's recent writings tend to gloss over the chaotic assemblages of alternative, grass roots networks, alliances, single-issue campaigns, online forums, community and self-help groups and so forth, that demand our critical attention. His recent work, given its emphasis, lacks the modicum of political and sociological realism required to make critical theory relevant to the concrete concerns and aspirations of many, many ordinary citizens who have long since given up on the hope of changing mainstream political culture and have scattered elsewhere to pursue more tangible projects. Greenpeace and Amnesty International are *not* necessarily the most relevant kinds of civil society initiative: in their fine grasp of administrative rationality and public relations, they rival their governmental and corporate counterparts. What is needed is not more analysis of the tensions and links between communicative and strategic rationality but, rather, more analysis of the tensions and links between communicative and *tactical* rationality in these localised spheres of activity.

Whether the shift in emphasis from the strategic towards the tactical in contemporary political culture is productive or retrograde is not quite the point here. Habermas cannot even begin to see how ordinary citizens might (re)engage communicatively, rather than opportunistically, with the official polity – be it at local, regional, national or supranational levels – if he does not take seriously the possibility that a critical mass of citizens is simply *not interested* in struggling to reform a set of structures so thoroughly external, remote and arcane in appearance. How, then, might we think beyond this fatalism? If a more vigorous public culture cannot be magically 'switched on', can we imagine it growing slowly from small beginnings? Might a political culture grow in confidence when citizens acquire experiences of 'making a difference' and seeing something of themselves in those micro-public spheres and small-scale initiatives? Or is political culture being irrevocably fractured by this drift? These questions are a blind spot in recent Habermasian theory. I have suggested that Habermas is putting the conceptual but *not necessarily* the historical cart before the horse in this endeavour partly because, in abstraction, we cannot prejudge the extent to which these micro-public spheres of discourse and action are already contributing to or detracting from the development of a more outward looking political culture: and partly because we would do well (and this is one saving grace of the recent Habermasian bias) to remember that a civil society *without* constitutional and legal guarantees is an impoverished and Darwinian one, so those large-scale constitutional issues can scarcely be dismissed as irrelevant. Nevertheless, it still turns out that, after all, there is too much globalism and not enough localism in recent Habermasian theory.

Then we might come to the question of evaluating the tactical turn in political culture. It's certainly beyond the scope of these pages to analyse the supposed gains and losses. But we must at least acknowledge the pervasive discourse of globalisation as the dispersal or decentring of power. The potentially mystifying aspect of this discourse – that it belies *increased* inequalities and consolidations of power – is deeply problematic. That globalisation makes for more mobile and complex *flows* of capital, information, culture, technology and people, and calls into question the efficacy of centralised, statist, and localised forms of regulation, is much harder to dispute.

The corollary has been a focus on decentred and fragmented cultural identities: the globalising mediascape, diaspora and migration, heightened concern with gender, sexual and ethnic identities – all these have helped to problematise the sociological norm of the self-identical, stable subject and shifted attention towards the instability, the contradictions, the complexities and the reflexive aspects of identity constitution in the contemporary world. Globalisation has shown itself to be an overwhelmingly entropic dynamic and the social sciences have been engaged in a project to develop new vocabularies and tropes that can help to map some of the new complexities: Manuel Castells' 'space of flows' in the 'network society';[76] Arjun Appadurai's topography of globalisation as 'financescapes', 'ideoscapes', 'ethnoscapes', 'mediascapes' and 'technoscapes';[77] MacKenzie Wark's 'virtual geographies' of the 'vector':[78] these are just some of the sociological attempts, each problematic in its own way, to engage the complexities of globalisation.

Yet Habermas, critical eyes trained on the problem of constitutionalism and citizenship with a capital C, displays a cavalier disregard for the decentred network tropes of recent social theory. Implicitly, Habermas's world seems to be one in which self-identical and centred citizens inhabit a series of totalities ordered as concentric circles and project their identities rather like stones thrown in a pond: the private *sphere* is not only co-original with, but is also *contained by* the public sphere; so too, the micro within the macro; the local within the national within the supranational within the global. In fact, this reductive 'Russian doll-ism' does not sit well with Habermas's own intersubjectivism, with his critique of the liberal model of the pre-political self, his explicit acknowledgement of a 'network model' of identity constitution,[79] or his emphasis in *The Theory of Communicative Action* on the importance of feminist and ecological movements in resisting the encroachment of administrative or corporate logic into areas of life where it is unwelcome – something which already hinted at decentred tactics and at the possibility that the term 'new social movement' would be misleading in its gesture towards lofty, stratospheric ambitions. It certainly does not sit well with the reality of geographic, cultural, occupational and informational mobilities (both enforced and voluntary) that have so many of today's citizens juggling memberships, responsibilities, affiliations and ontological 'locations'.

So why retreat back into the safety of a state-oriented model of centred, territorially anchored citizenship? One major factor must certainly be Habermas's own location in post-unification Germany demanding urgent debate on constitutional reform. One could also argue that the urgency of questions surrounding the role of law and the constitution within progressive politics has perhaps been obscured amid the social-scientific focus on globalisation *as* economic, political and cultural entropy: in that context, a reminder of the need to rethink the role of law and constitutionalism in a more nuanced way in order to address problems of justice and cultural recognition in an increasingly complex world may be a healthy antidote.

But taken on its own, Habermas's recent work retains a serious blind spot. This can only be addressed if critical theory pays attention to the question of whether micro-public spheres can overcome their parochialism in ways which are not necessarily centre-oriented. Where there is *no* centre as such, only differential clusterings of power, it makes no sense to pathologise or neglect those zones of discourse and activity that target one such nodal point at the expense of another. To reiterate, this is not to buy into the rather shortsighted anti-statism of some current protest movements and anarchistic subcultures, where the state is often dismissed not only as a potential force for good, but also as a minor player – a mere conduit for corporate power – in the world's ills. But not all roads do or should lead to the state – it is not the vanishing point of the dialectic of justice and solidarity, which is what we are in danger of gleaning from Habermas's later work, at least when we read it in isolation from his earlier writings. There are problems of justice and solidarity that implicate the constitutional state, but there are many zones of society in which advances in both can and must be pursued elsewhere. In its centring and privileging of the constitutional state, Habermas's particular batch of Hegelian tincture seems decidedly past its 'use by'.

One of the constraints Habermas places on his own recent critical theory is an exclusive concern with the problem of solidarity and justice between 'strangers', that is, people who wish to remain strangers but who seek common ground with the 'Others' to whom they are linked into networks of fate. There is a sense in which globalisation lends this project greater and greater urgency as we come to acknowledge the complex networks of interconnection that, regardless of our choosing, implicate us in expanding networks of difference. At the same time, this is a one-dimensional formulation. Solidarity and strangerdom are large and complex lands. For, as citizens, we tolerate and, at times, even crave different levels of proximity to our 'neighbours'. To be 'good' citizens in a pluralistic world, we certainly must follow

Habermas's injunction to aspire to unconditional respect for our neighbours – we must respect each other's differences even as we try to establish common grounds for dialogue.

But the bonds of solidarity that we seek in the public sphere may at times be simultaneously thicker *and* thinner than Habermas's constitutional model implies: thicker because we often seek friendship and familiarity, deep levels of trust, people to laugh with and get angry with, people who we can engage in passionate argument – the kinds of relations we develop with others *because* of who they are and not *despite* who they are (a theme we discussed in Chapter 1); but thinner precisely because the decentred citizen does not put all her existential eggs into one basket, does not – perhaps could not – be transparently self-identical in any given space. The totalising and pessimistic prognosis is that citizens of a fragmented and pluralistic society only find these thickened-out bonds of solidarity within relatively closed family, friendship or cultural groups. But the realities of a protest movement, an online discussion group, a web-log community or a local self-help group often show this to be a partial truth. Micro-public spheres are rarely free of visible exclusionary or parochial characteristics. Yet frequently they do bring together strange bedfellows, be it the anarchists and the elderly women joined in protest against the building of a new highway, or the US and Iraqi 'bloggers' finding points of empathy and common interest whilst their fundamental world-views remain poles apart. The decentred self opens up possibilities for thickened, if more ad hoc and transient, bonds of solidarity to develop between 'Others' than Habermas's rather dry model of constitutional patriotism allows for.

There is an irony here. Habermas is frequently criticised for fetishising *dialogue* at the expense of one-way and mass mediated communication (something I will take up the following chapter) and for privileging the ideal of *co-presence* between citizens in the guise of the 'ideal speech situation' at the expense of the scattered 'imagined community'. And yet here is this champion of *proximity* formulating a model – indeed, an ethic – of citizenship whose mantra seems to be 'keep your distance!', lest the 'integrity' of the Other be damaged; 'include the Other', might run the small print, 'but do not expect too much of her and do not give too much of yourself'. In *The Theory of Communicative Action* Habermas drew heavily on Lawrence Kohlberg's idea of 'post-conventional' morality, which privileges interaction between 'generalised Others' over that between 'concrete Others', something which Carol Gilligan had forcefully argued to be a male-centric model of morality, favouring relations of 'justice' over relations of 'care'.[80] Habermas now conceives the dialectic of solidarity and justice as something which demands of citizens a *simultaneous* orientation towards the generalised and the concrete Other. But, at best, he want us to apply only a thin crust of constitutional concrete and still does not seem to take rich interpersonal bonds and relationships as seriously relevant to the public sphere.

Habermas's model does not really allow for the rich encounters of difference that could meet his own demand for a sufficiently concrete and motivating public culture; it does not allow for rich connectivities between 'Others' that can develop – with work and with mishaps along the way – without shattering the integrity of our mutual otherness. He seems to treat identity as if it were some delicate glass ball of singularity, to buy into Habermas's own telling penchant for spherical metaphors. It does not allow for what Donna Haraway, who shares with Habermas a mistrust of identity politics (they share little else), has called a 'politics of affinity'[81] between citizens who find and mutually reconfigure points of connection or common ground. In stark contrast to Haraway's ethic of solidarity, Habermas, despite emphasising the rationalisation and reflexivity of the lifeworld, ends up foregrounding a politics of *boundary maintenance*. The point here is not to totalise or unequivocally celebrate the 'decentred citizen': some citizens will be more 'decentred' than others (though affluence and privilege are not the only determinants); and decentred identities can yield vulnerability and anxieties as well as the advantages of multiple social connectivities. Nor is the point to embrace the wholesale collapse of boundaries as Haraway is wont to do. But it is to argue for a more open conception of citizenship *and* solidarity than Habermas provides. And it is to argue for a critical theory that seriously considers the decentred activist networks for whom tactics prevail over strategy and for whom the rhizome,[82] rather than the acorn and the oak tree, is the operative metaphor; the 'Buy Nothing' day campaigns and the culture jammers; but also the online networks; the neighbourhood watch groups; the single-issue campaigns of local communities; the self-help groups; the new religious groups; the xenophobic campaigns trying to prevent asylum seekers being housed in a local community; refugee support groups; the cellular terrorist network; hacker groups; the whole gamut of diverse, contradictory but decentred micro-publics and networks that increasingly comprise the political life of civil society. Habermas would perhaps lament this chaotic assemblage as symptomatic of a fractured, and not simply decentred, public culture. But critical theory needs to address the localisation, the diversification, the fuzzy boundaries and the decentring of public life if it is to remain relevant to the contemporary world.

4
Mediations: From the Coffee House to the Internet Café

Media institutions and technologies shouldered the burden of extreme hopes, expectations and fears throughout the twentieth century, and this shows little sign of abating in the digitised twenty-first. From the point of view of democracy and citizenship, the media have in some quarters been painted as agents of depoliticisation and mass consumerism, and as harbingers of better democracy in others; they are expected to expose, hold to account and dilute power; or they are vilified for their distortions and deflections. The pervasive role of mediated communication in contemporary social, political and cultural life is, however, rarely in dispute.

It's necessary for any serious investigation of the public sphere to foreground the issue of mediation. This is something Habermas has been rightly criticised for failing to do. As I touched on in the first chapter, there is an implicit logocentrism lurking in Habermas's theoretical frameworks, an unproblematised communications hierarchy that privileges speech and the printed word. In *Structural Transformation*, the electronic and audio-visual media were greeted with a certain contempt: in Habermas's subsequent writing they became little more than an afterthought, encapsulated in the vague claim that they represent a 'compromise' between a dialogically conceived communicative action and the non-discursive steering media of the 'system'.[1] In the absence of any serious investigation of the role of communications media, *The Theory of Communicative Action* suggests a problematic binary between action 'mediated' by non-discursive steering media, on the one hand, and 'unmediated' discourse, on the other. Now, this is clearly not Habermas's intention. He knows that even speech *is* mediation – he has taken the linguistic turn, even if he has not followed his post-structuralist counterparts down quite the same road. Habermas doesn't subscribe to the fallacy of transparent communication. In order to address this tension, we need to assess, first, whether Habermas's theory actually falls over when it confronts the realities of pervasive mediation in the contemporary world; and second, what kind of critical purchase, if any, it offers for dealing with extant modes of mediated communication. I aim to provide an introduction to these questions in this chapter. I'll conclude by suggesting not simply that the Habermasian public-sphere framework can and must *accommodate* the realities of pervasive mediation but that if it were to *critically embrace* mediation it would be a greatly enriched framework.

Unlike John Durham Peters,[2] then, who elegantly critiques the tendency for communications theory (Habermas included) to privilege the Socratic ideals of *dialogue* and *reciprocity* over the model of scattered, one-to-many communications, my argument is oriented instead towards deconstructing the binary of mediated ('bad') and unmediated ('good') communication. Like Peters, I will also begin by discussing mediation as *mass* mediation. But I will then move on to a broader definition of mediation, one that encompasses putatively dialogic media forms (implicating so-called 'new' media in particular), but one which also encourages us to think of mediation as something other than simply a tradeoff between intersubjective discourse and the non-discursive influences of money and power.

THE FALL OF THE *AGORA*

Probably the crispest critique of the Habermasian public sphere as a media-blind anachronism was developed by John B. Thompson.[3] What distinguishes Thompson's critique from others that target the logocentrism of the Habermasian public sphere[4] is the way it retains Habermas's focus on the democratic imagination and the problems of legitimacy and power in contemporary society. Because it raises such salient issues, I shall devote some space to it here. Thompson calls on those concerned with the problem of democracy to bid a fond farewell to that cherished dream, an arena of dialogical public deliberation and participation which nostalgically gestures back to the citizens' assemblies of the ancient Greek *agora* and to an idealistic symbiosis of *lexis* and *praxis*, word and deed. Where the Greeks sought to create reciprocal speech relations (among male slave-owning citizens) coterminous with the social space over which decisions impacted, the problem for democrats in the modern world is of a radically different order. 'We live in a world today', Thompson reminds us, 'in which the sheer scale and complexity of decision-making processes limits the extent to which they can be organised in a participatory way.'[5] Modern 'communities of fate' are too large and too complex, and the consequences of political and economic decisions are too diffuse, for the classical model of democracy to be of significant value in the contemporary world, even as a counterfactual ideal.

> There are, of course, many areas of social life in which individuals could assume a greater role in decision-making processes, and it may be the case that increased participation in these processes would facilitate the formation of what Habermas calls 'public opinion'. But at the level of national and international politics, and at the upper levels in which power is exercised in large-scale civil and commercial organizations, *it is difficult to see how the idea of participatory opinion formation could be implemented in any significant way*. What we may hope for at best is a greater diffusion of information concerning the activities of powerful individuals and organizations, a greater diversity in channels of diffusion and a greater emphasis on the establishment of mechanisms through which these activities can be rendered accountable and controlled.[6]

As a simple rejection of participatory models of democracy, there is scarcely anything controversial in this. From hard-nosed technocratic elitism through to reluctant realism, democratic theory has long concerned itself with the limits of democratic participation in modern, complex societies. Debates have emphasised time constraints, the imperatives of efficiency and expertise, the specialisation of expert knowledge, and the rights of citizens to a private life protected from the tyranny of an over-politicised society. What's interesting about Thompson's arguments, however – and what concerns us here – is the way in which he draws upon the prevalence of communications media to criticise Habermas and to reinforce the case against participatory models of democracy. The arguments Thompson advances suggest at least five related ways in which the Habermasian account of the public sphere abstracts itself from the realities of the contemporary world. Thompson is concerned to show that Habermas's dialogical model fails to account for (1) the precise nature of mass-mediated communication and (2) the role it plays in contemporary social life. He suggests further that the dialogical model fails to account for the way the mass media constitute interaction (3) between citizens and decision makers and (4) amongst citizens themselves, as co-participants in processes of public-opinion formation. Thompson then suggests (5) that Habermas's model of public space provides a skewed understanding of the prospects for more democratic forms of social organisation and demonstrates, at best, a limited understanding of the role of a reconstructed media space in the realisation of those prospects. I shall touch on each of these issues in turn.

(1) According to Thompson, the rise of communications media ushered in an era characterised by the ascendancy of 'mediated quasi-interaction'.[7] Where face-to-face interaction occurs in a common physical locale and may in principle gesture towards reciprocal speech relations, communications media have enabled the 'disembedding' of social relations which is characteristic of modernity, where interaction is uprooted from shared spatial and temporal contexts. Thompson distinguishes two types of mediated interaction. One type (for example, telephony, e-mail or letter-writing) facilitates dialogic encounters across space and/or time (although it also reconfigures face-to-face interaction, engendering new conventions, constraints and opportunities).[8] By contrast, 'mediated *quasi*-interaction' describes institutionalised communication which is not analogous to the dialogical encounter:

> there are two key respects in which mediated quasi-interaction differs from both face-to-face interaction and mediated interaction. In the first place, the participants in face-to-face interaction and mediated interaction are oriented towards specific others, for whom they produce utterances, expressions, etc.; but in the case of mediated quasi-interaction, symbolic forms are produced for an indefinite range of potential recipients. Second, whereas face-to-face interaction and mediated interaction are dialogical, mediated quasi-interaction is monological in character, in the sense that the flow of communication is predominantly one way ... But mediated quasi-interaction is, none the less, a form of interaction ... It is a structured situation in which some individuals are engaged primarily in producing symbolic forms for others who are not physically present, while others are involved primarily in receiving symbolic forms produced by others to whom they cannot respond, but with whom they can form bonds of friendship, affection or loyalty.[9]

(2) In privileging dialogue, Habermas also fails to account for the increasing prevalence of media and the role they play in contemporary social and political life. Thompson's thesis is not that mediated quasi-interaction replaces face-to-face interaction. He recognises that it serves to stimulate and inform localised dialogue, that media products, that is, become the subject of 'discursive elaboration'[10] – a process of fundamental importance to Habermas's narrative of the bourgeois public sphere. But neither, in that case, does it merely supplement older forms of social interaction.[11] The rise of mass

communications is implicated in a radical *transformation* of social relations. The development of complex modern societies signals the rise of social interconnections (both between individuals and institutions and between citizens themselves) which are increasingly underscored by *absence* rather than presence; where interaction is *mediated* through monetary exchange, through bureaucratic administration, *and* through communications technologies and media forms. Lifeworlds are shot through with the consequences of actions whose authors are physically (and often cognitively) absent. A citizen's economic life can be rendered sensible, that is, amenable to a degree of 'cognitive mapping',[12] only in the context of a vast network of distant forces which, together, constitute the economic totality; consumption connects the individual to a plethora of distant production contexts; and freedoms are bounded by coercive measures legislated by distant social actors. Similarly, the citizen is confronted with action *choices* (as consumer or worker, voter or activist, etc.) that will be consequential for others with whom, once again, no direct or dialogical interaction will ever ensue.

Communications technologies allow citizens some element of connectivity with the physically absent actors and social processes through which their experiences and action choices are structured. For the pre-moderns, absent sources of power – such as the expansive rule of monarchs and churches – were bound to remain largely invisible as well as impermeable. With the dispersion of communications technologies, the situation is radically different. These technologies enhance the potential to 'work through' the linkages between a locally situated lifeworld and the intrusion of a world 'out there', whilst *creating* new distantiated relations through the dissemination of symbols: 'lived experience' and 'mediated experience' are progressively interwoven.[13]

The Habermasian model of public space, however, woefully underplays the role of 'mediated quasi-interaction'. Possibilities for democratic 'connectivity' are in large part shaped by *mass* media. Where mediated interaction disembeds dialogue and, in doing so, can help to counteract the consequences of *physical distance* (though I shall later argue that this is only a partial account),[14] mediated quasi-interaction rarely serves the function of simply negating absence or abolishing distance. Media channels engage with the problem of societal complexity, constituting new modes of interaction based on *visibility*: media personnel occupy the *specialist* role of selecting, processing and producing vast networks of symbols and significant information (they are gatekeepers and agenda setters), discursively interrogating decision makers (they serve as advocates), and making accessible the world 'out there' (or, rather, selecting segments and constructing versions of it) on behalf of a more or less diffuse audience.

(3) As filtered networks of visibility and 'quasi-interactive' encounters, media institutions and technologies constitute the sine qua non of a democratic public culture in modern complex societies. But Habermas's theory of the public sphere is found wanting when it comes to an understanding of the types of interaction that the media institute between citizens and decision makers or public figures. In modern democratic societies, systems of representative democracy emerge precisely because societal complexity dictates a division of labour between the specialised roles of decision makers, on the one hand, and a diffuse citizenry as a source of legitimation, on the other. Media *configure* that division of labour in a specific way. They produce, gather, process and distribute information and discourse; they engender 'visibility' by painting or sketching, rather than simply revealing, public figures and social processes. But societal complexity limits the scope for challenging hierarchies of expert knowledge and the media fulfill an essential function as they filter, configure, compress and render accessible for the lay citizen vast and complex networks of information and accountability. Selective visibility, by definition, prohibits the emergence of communicative transparency: the mass media do not serve as a window on the inner workings of each and every significant decision-making process: the mediated transmission of information and expert knowledge and the scope for 'discursively testing' the claims of public figures are curtailed by limits to *supply* (factors include technical constraints, the available quantity of media space etc.) and by limits to *demand* (factors include citizens' free time, motivation, etc.). The democratic imagination is often reluctant to acknowledge that the demeanour, the image and the reputations of public figures are the symbolic tokens in which a highly mediated public culture primarily deals.

In a world of complex, specialised decision-making processes, democracy, we might say, is founded not upon communicative transparency but upon the establishment of channels of visibility through which feelings of 'trust' and 'mistrust' circulate. 'Trust', in this sense, implies a balancing act between acquiring knowledge and understanding of decision-making processes and investing a degree of *faith* in the integrity, acumen and expertise of decision makers. 'Trust', as Anthony Giddens puts it, 'is related to absence in time and space. There would be no need to trust anyone whose activities were continually visible ... All trust is in a sense blind trust.'[15] The media constitute us as citizens by offering us *processed* insights into an array of significant domains – economic, political, scientific and so forth – through which democratic choices and opinions can emerge, and not by breaching the boundaries between decision makers and those on the receiving end of their decisions. According to this view, Habermas's theories misguidedly encourage us to dismiss questions of image and repute as mere communicative distortions, or to understand them in terms of a 'refeudalisation' of the public sphere. In so doing, the Habermasian model has no means of engaging critically with what is an intrinsic and vital dimension of the democratic process.

In this reading, the key problem for contemporary democracy is *not* how society *presents* or, via communications media, *re*presents itself, but, rather, *how we communicate with the absent.*[16] Habermas, it seems, may have been barking up the wrong tree. If Thompson's emphasis on 'trust' reflects his concern with the problems of democracy and legitimation, he also acknowledges the range of different 'connectivities' that can be engendered by mediated quasi-interaction, including feelings of love, hatred, sexual attraction or intimacy that can be projected onto public figures. What's interesting here is that Thompson constructs a sociological discourse that differs greatly from the post-structuralist critique of reason usually invoked against Habermas. Thompson's is a rather pragmatic (and, as I shall suggest, perhaps even utilitarian) discourse that is poles apart from the anti-foundationalist and politically abstracted tenor of most post-structuralist discourse. Yet it still winds up by highlighting the dangers of treating, as Habermas tends to do, the condensations, aestheticisations, ellipses, spectacles and intensities of mediated communication as creases that can be progressively ironed out instead of seeing in them the very texture and fabric of contemporary public life.

(4) The media play a crucial role not only in mediating between the citizenry and the various loci of decision-making power but also in constituting interactions between citizens themselves. The suspicion must be that Habermas's model of the public sphere is to be found wanting here as well. The configuration and dissemination of symbols and cultural forms through the media facilitate the development of identities that draw upon discourses of nationhood, ethnicity, class,

gender, style or taste subcultures, opinion and political affiliation, interest group, status group, identification with public figures and so forth. The public sphere is, of course, also a site of conflict and contradiction in which particular world-views, tastes, aspirations and opinions clash with one another. It constitutes space in which feelings of intense antipathy, as well as identification, are evoked. Democratic citizenship remains dependent, nevertheless, upon *membership*, however abstract, of a shared social space in which conflicting opinions and identities can interact with one another. In a pluralistic society, a sense of membership or of belonging to a political community is not, as we discussed in the previous chapter, conditional on buying into a monolithic or homogeneous identity, but does depend on the extent to which the public sphere is perceived as inclusive and representative by its diverse citizenry.

However, the ways in which the media situate citizens within the public sphere seem, once again, to have only a limited affinity with the dialogical ideals of Habermas's model of public discourse. Large-scale modern publics are 'imagined communities' precisely because we interact directly with just a fraction of our fellow citizens. Again, the media facilitate those connections, *on the citizenry's behalf*, through the configuration and dissemination of symbols and the selective staging of public debate and cultural encounter. The feelings of antipathy or identification evoked by media symbols are not, for the most part, conveyed back to the producers of those symbols. They are, instead, refracted into localised contexts. Similarly, the extent to which citizens experience themselves as *members* of a political community depends on the depth of a largely *imagined* bond: the extent to which various citizens see themselves as included in or excluded by the 'communality' of watching a televised event of 'national significance', or the ritual reading of the morning papers along with millions of absent others, for example. We should point out also, the increasing scope for participating in *displaced* 'imagined communities' such that migrants, diaspora and travellers can opt to read the morning papers from their home country on the Internet, or cheer their home nation in a televised sporting event. An increasingly globalised mediascape makes it increasingly, though differentially, possible for citizens to selectively opt in and out of specific imagined communities.

In other words, Thompson points to a serious lacuna in Habermas's historical account of the public sphere. In framing the development of the press during the seventeenth and eighteenth centuries as an *extension* of the critical debates taking place in Europe's salons and coffee houses (and in characterising the later development of the broadcast media and more commercialised, larger-scale print media as an 'historical fall from grace'), Habermas obscures the fact that the development of mass printing actually heralded the waning significance of public *dialogue*. The very emergence of a politically active public within complex, differentiated and politically centralised societies was only possible with the rise of *mass* printing which, by definition, dealt in the diffuse circulation of information and symbols, targeted towards relatively anonymous and generic audiences, and which was characterised by a radical separation and numerical disparity between *producers* and *receivers*, that is, by the dynamic of *specialisation*. The eighteenth-century publics that Habermas cautiously celebrated may have engaged in critical dialogue *within specific localised contexts* (such as the coffee house) but, taken as a whole – and in contrast to the Greek *polis* – they were engaged in the project of building *imagined* communities.[17]

(5) Thompson is well aware that in Habermasian critical theory, discourse ethics have a counterfactual status and serve as a means of gaining some critical purchase on the shortcomings of extant communications. Yet, for him, this really constitutes a theoretical and political 'red herring' because, in its utopian attachment to the dilution of power and to the ideals of reciprocity, it has little to tell us about real issues concerning the *distribution* and *legitimation* of power, the possibility of constructing more effective modes of *representative* democracy and the manner in which communications media might realistically serve to make power relations and decision-making processes more visible and accountable in complex, differentiated societies.

Thompson has no trouble finding common ground with the 'radical democrat' media theorists[18] who, largely inspired by Habermas's *Structural Transformation*, have argued strenuously for pluralistic and decentred public service media institutions that are funded but not governed by the state, and which can serve as independent bulwarks against the pervasive commodification of the mediascape (internationally, few such institutions – even the noble BBC – have scored well on *both* counts simultaneously). But he also alerts us to a more realistic and focused view of the potential democratisation of the media. For in *navigating* (rather than dissolving) the gulf between specialist decision-making spheres and the citizenry, vital *specialist* functions accrue to media personnel themselves. As citizens, audiences are asked to invest a large degree of *faith* in the way media institutions select, gather, construct and configure information and symbols on their behalf. Citizens are dependent on media personnel to render a complex world at least partially accessible, and to disseminate information and symbols proficiently and responsibly.

It could easily be objected that Thompson's critique and alternative emphasis misses the increasingly digitised mediascape that was emerging at the time he was developing it. With the benefit of hindsight, it might look like a discourse that belongs to the analogue era, privileging *mass* media at the expense of the myriad interactive, niche and DIY media forms that have since become pervasive. But although I will return to the realm of the digital in the following section, I think this really misses the point. One of the serious pitfalls of all the millennial huff and puff around digitisation and the Internet characteristic of the past decade has been precisely that it privileges questions of access to the means of expression and the distribution of 'discourse chances'. Thompson's pragmatic corrective to Habermas is a timely reminder that in order to assess the democratic dimensions of the mediascape, we must in fact avoid an exclusive focus on either the wondrous potentials *or* the existent shortcomings of public access and interactivity, whether it's manifested in the various DIY media sweeping the Internet, the rise and rise of talk radio and reality TV in broadcasting, or the ersatz 'interactivities' of 'narrowcasting', media-on-demand, and the digital 'me channel'.[19] The empires of Murdoch and Berlusconi; the narrowness of the CNN and BBC world-views; the massive entertainment, news and advertising synergies in the global mediascape: in the digital age, these things all face an array of competitors for the critical attentions of communication scholars, but they most certainly are *not* relics of an analogue 'mass communications' era in terminal decline.

We continue to live with *and to depend upon* dizzyingly huge and opaque media complexes. As with the other 'expert systems' which we expect the media to shed some light on, the extent to which the media themselves could be organised in a participatory fashion remains strictly limited. Rather than visualising the media simply as a deterritorialised *agora* writ large, democrats must look beyond classical ideals and engage with the fact that, collectively at least, immense power accrues to the media. That this power could never simply be dissolved, and that the democratic project therefore demands imaginative but realistic proposals to improve media accountability and diversity, is all but lost in the utopian vision of the public sphere driven by the ideals of unbounded reciprocity. Thompson's corrective is certainly a useful one. There are, however, some blind spots contained within it.

The central role modernity carves out for 'mediated publicness' is double-edged. The overwhelmingly negative conclusions which Habermas drew in his early work on the rise of a mass-mediated public sphere, Thompson claims, are shortsighted and politically impotent.[20] Habermas characterises the increasing ubiquity of the mass media (especially the broadcast media) in terms of a 'refeudalisation of the public sphere' such that the 'principle of publicity' undergoes a transformation away from reasoned critical debate towards its contemporary association with public relations and marketing techniques.

> In the measure that it is shaped by public relations, the public sphere of civil society again takes on feudal features. The 'suppliers' display a showy pomp before customers ready to follow. Publicity initiates the kind of aura proper to the personal prestige and supernatural authority once bestowed by the kind of publicity involved in [feudal] representation.[21]

Thompson criticises Habermas's 'refeudalisation thesis' on a number of grounds. Whilst the prevalence of mediated quasi-interaction may offer political leaders and dominant groups new possibilities for engaging in calculated political marketing, slick presentation and rehearsed 'debate', it also creates new threats to the strategic successes of political communication.[22] In comparison with print, electronic media certainly lend themselves to different – often more frenetic and less sober or contemplative – temporalities (though this thesis can be overstated if we consider, for example, the rather rigid temporalities and daily production cycles of the traditional daily newspaper against the way in which many digital media accrue automated archival and non-linear retrieval functions). Broadcasters, for instance, may largely control the timing, pace and rhythms at which media messages are transmitted (time-shifting consumer gadgets such as VCR or TiVo have dented but not eliminated this scheduling function) in a way which sets electronic broadcasting apart from print media. But unlike the 'representative publicness' characteristic of the feudal era, the break between speaker and hearer also limits the control media personnel or public figures themselves exercise over factors such as the reception context or audience composition.[23] In addition, new media technologies progressively erode the control politicians and

leaders exercise over the dividing line between desired and damaging visibility. The relentless pursuit of publicity carries with it serious risks: 'Gaffes and outbursts, performances which backfire and scandals are some of the ways in which the limits of control are most clearly and strikingly manifested.'[24] This has never been truer than with the rise of the Internet, which makes the job of information managers harder (and their salaries higher!) than ever.

This certainly provides an important counterweight to some of the monolithic excesses which characterise Habermas's early work. However, Thompson's account does little to clarify the distinction between the ambivalent *potential* of mediated quasi-interaction, on the one hand, and the manner in which power holders have actually sought, with varying degrees of success, to minimise the risks associated with it. Direct and indirect mechanisms of censorship and misinformation do not feature strongly in Thompson's analysis. Many democrats would vehemently resist, for example, Thompson's suggestion that the 1991 Gulf War exemplified the way in which 'the exercise of political power takes place in an arena which is increasingly open to view' and 'global scrutiny'.[25] In the eyes of many, it provided the occasion for the most cynical and large-scale manipulation of the Western media ever seen (rivalled only by subsequent instalments). This raises the question, 'What *kind* of visibility?'[26] Edward Said, with some justification, described the Gulf War as 'the most *covered* and the least *reported* war in history'.[27] Witnessing the subsequent drip-feed revelations about the misinformation deployed during the Gulf War, or sitting in front of Michael Moore's *Fahrenheit 9/11*, two years on from the Twin Towers, one is reminded of the immense counter-hegemonic *struggles* that have to be waged in order for the dominant frames to be *unsettled*, let alone overturned.

Just *how* the media construct public discourse – whether they inform or misinform, whether they contextualise events, and whether they focus on substantive issues or simply on the cosmetics of public relations and personality politics – relates to a broader question about the political system as a whole and constitutes, I suggest, a second problem with Thompson's thesis. This stems from the rather vague notion of 'risk' that he employs. That mediated quasi-interaction creates certain risks for visible public figures is undeniable. What is less certain is that this somehow endows the public with greater mechanisms of control with which to hold power relations and decision-making processes in check. The reason Habermas's refeudalisation thesis may be of more value than his critics tend to assume is that in *The Structural Transformation of the Public Sphere*, Habermas is *not*, as Thompson alleges, concerned solely with 'a relatively superficial aspect of politics – namely, the cultivation of image and the preoccupation with showy presentation',[28] but also with the dynamics that, in late modernity, obstruct the development of independent spaces of deliberation within civil society through the unchecked expansion of administrative and corporate logic, and the hollowing out of formal arenas of democratic deliberation. The 'risks' to which Thompson refers will often have more to do with the precarious careers of individual public figures than with the vulnerability of societal power structures.

Neither of these ambiguities, however, detract from Thompon's central thesis, namely that where large-scale decision-making processes are at stake, democratic citizenship presupposes large-scale (which is *not* to say, centralised) networks of mediated visibility. Contemporary patterns of globalisation serve to reinforce such an assertion. As socio-economic and cultural connectivities stretch ever further beyond the parameters of the nation state, democrats are faced with the daunting task of imagining new institutions (including media systems) which can hold increasingly globalised power relations in check. Can a democratic media system (such as the public service broadcasting model exemplified by the BBC) confer genuine rights of citizenship if it remains rooted to a *national* political arena whose sovereignty is under increasing strain? It is true that the increased pressures upon the nation state should not be confused with the *end* of the nation state, given the abiding significance of the national political arena, the many renaissances of nationalism and protectionism, and – obvious but crucial to media policy debates – the commonplace (though not universal) congruence between linguistic and national territorial boundaries.[29] And yet the problems and issues which citizens face today – complex global inequalities, environmental issues, the arms industries, terrorist networks or human rights, for example – cannot be confined to the national arena of public deliberation and policy formation. For radical democrats, the complexities this brings to media policy debates are immense. Along which dimensions should democratic media systems be constructed? How are they to be funded and constitutionally protected? How are the funding bodies and media systems themselves to be held accountable? How are linguistic and cultural barriers to be addressed? How do media systems deal with the incongruence between economic, cultural and political patterns of globalisation?

For Nicholas Garnham, however, the aspirations of the democratic imagination, however utopian, must be conceived in straightforward terms even amid this daunting complexity:

> In short, the problem is to construct systems of democratic accountability integrated with media systems of matching scale that occupy the same social space as that over which economic or political decisions will impact. If the impact is universal, then both the political and media systems must be universal. In this sense, a series of autonomous public spheres is not sufficient. There must be a single public sphere, even if we might want to conceive of this single public sphere as made up of a series of subsidiary public spheres, each organized around its own political structure, media system, and set of norms and interests. Thus even if we accept that debate within the public sphere is riven with controversy and in many instances may be directed at agreeing to disagree rather than toward consensus, we are still faced with the unavoidable problem of translating debate into action.[30]

In the context of globalisation, however, Garnham's vision of a global public sphere is susceptible to the dangers of a bad universalism, namely one that takes the universal as the foundation rather than the orientation of diversified public discourses. That would be to neglect the uneven and entropic consequences of globalisation including, of course, an increasing vocalisation of demands for greater political and cultural autonomy.[31] A radical democratic framework which seeks to link the mediascape to questions of empowerment points up the need to envisage, *in tandem*, the role of both particular micro-publics, where experiences, identities, inequalities and differences can be articulated in diverse, irregular, and relatively open ways, and more universal channels, where those diverse discourses and cultural forms might encounter each other in common communicative space.

A key premise of Thompson's perspective can be summarised as follows:

> Social life is made up of individuals who pursue aims and objectives within social contexts that are structured in certain ways. In pursuing their objectives, individuals draw on the resources available to them; these resources are the means which enable them to pursue their aims and interests effectively, and thereby to exercise some degree of power.[32]

But what of the *contexts* in which those aims and objectives actually develop? If we accept that individuals do not exist in a vacuum but within the symbolic networks through which identities and aspirations emerge, then how are we to critically distinguish between different symbolic contexts? Are citizens simply conceived as opportunists, strategically motivated individuals whose aims and interests are worked through within a relatively closed private domain and largely fixed prior to engaging in the public arena? Is the process of opinion formation *public* only to the extent that the mass media facilitate *quasi*-interaction and *imagined* bonds with absent others? Or is there some value to be gained from envisaging more spaces of public dialogue in which citizens' values, and not just those of public figures, are subjected to 'discursive testing', in which, in other words, public discourse, though it may never actually settle into comfortable (and dangerous!) consensus, still constitutes something other than the mere aggregate of privately (or 'quasi-publicly'!) generated opinions, feelings or desires? These are the questions Habermas's critical theory seeks to pose, in constrast to the rather reductivist and, ultimately, utilitarian framework sketched by Thompson.

> [The] struggle over the increasing *de-moralization of public conflicts* is in full swing. This no longer takes place under the sign of a technocratic conception of society and politics; where society has become so complex as to be a closed book, only opportunistic behaviour towards the system seems to offer a way of finding one's bearings. However, large-scale problems actually confronting the developed societies are scarcely such that they could be resolved without a mode of perception sensitive to normative demands, without a reintroduction of moral considerations into the issues under public discussion ... These problems can only be brought to a head by rethinking topics morally, by universalising interests in a more or less discursive manner in the form of liberal political cultures which have not been stripped of all their powers ... It helps to perceive the way one's own interests are bound up with the interests of others. The moral or ethical point of view makes us quicker to perceive the more far-reaching *and simultaneously less insistent and more fragile* ties that bind the fate of one individual to that of every other – making even the most alien person a member of one's community.[33]

According to this argument, then, even large-scale problems can only be 're-moralised' in a more or less 'bottom-up' fashion anchored in varied modes of *discourse*. The objection that localism necessarily implies parochialism and insularity is, as I intimated in the previous chapter, of limited validity here. Lifeworlds will, of course, always be rooted in time, and in physical, social and, we should add, *mediated*, space. But in the context of increasingly unstable horizons (a context shaped through media technologies, through travel, and the like), any *essential* link between localism and parochialism is eroded.

Parochialism can be sustained by both lifeworld and system dynamics. One entails the active resistance of participants to the increasing porosity of modern lifeworlds, which derives from living, working and travelling in a variety of different contexts, the cultural heterogeneity of geographical locales, and the reception of media symbols. The increased global mobility of symbols and cultural forms frequently presents itself as a *threat* to the narrative coherence of identities and heritage and not simply as an *opportunity* to embrace the diversity and flux of a deterritorialised cosmopolis. The systemic factors commonly include such phenomena as cultural protectionist policies (which is not the same as saying that all state support and protection for indigeneous culture actually promotes or aims to promote parochialism), government and/or commercially sponsored 'nation building' (emphasising heritage, patriotism or xenophobia, for example) in education and the cultural industries, socially divisive urban planning (for which the gated community is the operative metonym), or the unintended consequences of economic and technological developments that promote greater consumer choice and 'bespoke' media and cultural goods. What is certain is that withdrawal into fundamentalisms, ethnic nationalisms and insular localisms arises as a reaction to, and thus as a consequence of, contemporary globalisation, and is not simply a festering residue of an earlier age. But the extent to which globalisation elicits those reactions rather than the opening out of cultural and discursive boundaries is an empirical rather than a theoretical question. We could easily adduce numerous illustrations of both the centrifugal *and* centripetal consequences of globalisation. And yet the increasing vigour (and violence) with which so many groups and communities seek to police their symbolic and/or physical boundaries is the corollary of a reorganisation of space which sees the continual growth in *potential* for localised, critical discourse between participants who inhabit intersecting, rather than homogeneous, lifeworlds.

The communications media are critical in destabilising cultural boundaries and thus eroding that *essential* link between localised discourse and parochialism. In doing so, however, the large-scale media also reveal their own limitations. For it's difficult to see how either the exclusivism of imagined bonds, as in an ethnically conceived nationhood, or the ethnocentrism (and hollow abstractions) of universalising *ideas* (for that is all they are) such as 'humanity', the 'cosmopolis' or an ethic of 'global responsibility', could be significantly challenged or unsettled were citizens to depend *solely* upon those large-scale media for 'imagined' encounters with 'Others' and to 'discursively elaborate' those media symbols only within the confines of a homogenous, privatised lifeworld.

Whilst Habermas, since *Structural Transformation*, has been notoriously vague and unforthcoming on the nature and democratic role of communications media, Craig Calhoun has proposed a corrective that accords them their rightful place within Habermas's system–lifeworld framework. His thesis is that large-scale communications media are crucial for establishing shared interpretative frameworks (including stereotypes), for condensing and filtering information, and for granting citizens a degree of access to communities with which they are otherwise connected only via abstract systems, enabling them to make informed choices within the system of representative democracy. Calhoun is at pains to highlight the limitations of communitarian thought, which is prone to underplay the structural limitations of participatory democracy, to dismiss the problem of societal complexity and to treat the system in lifeworld terms: 'This is the fundamental misrecognition built into the bulk of localist, populist politics today.'[34]

However, there is a sense in which Calhoun tries to achieve the impossible: that is, to slot the mass media neatly into the system–lifeworld model and use it as a kind of neutral bridge between two separate domains. There are, I think, a number of problems with this approach. Because he deals only with the communications media in relation to systemic or 'large-scale' societal integration, he obscures the role they play in day-to-day lived experience, the way the global *becomes* part of the local. Large-scale media play a significant role in the 'uprooting' and differentiation of modern lifeworlds. This is not the place to engage with the vast literature on media reception:[35] suffice it to say that studies show modes and contexts of reception, patterns of demand, the background experiences and expectations brought into the reception context and the ways media products are 'used' as cultural and discursive scaffolds *in everyday life*, to be extremely diverse and complex. To neglect these local–global interactions is unwittingly to reinforce precisely the static and culturally segmented notion of 'community' characteristic of communitarian thinking. Such an account, then, provides no tools for distinguishing between conservative and progressive localisms and, crucially, neglects the role of large-scale communications media in 'stirring up' and reconfiguring localised lifeworlds, destabilising cultural boundaries and eroding the internal coherence of geographically bounded communities. The way in which media symbols feed into localised sites of discourse and deliberation is largely obscured and we are left with both a problematic conceptual binary (between what is 'internal' and what is 'external' to a cultural community) and a reductive political binary (between localisms concerned with purely local issues and a purely representative and mass-mediated political system designed to deal with large-scale problems). The image of a less rigidly conceived 'bottom-up' political culture, in which localised discourses feed into those representative structures, is lost, as too is the critical purchase we need to gain on large-scale communications media as simultaneously of (and not simply *between*) both 'system' *and* 'lifeworld'.

What is clear, though, is that the democratic imagination demands that we do not demonise large-scale and professionalised media simply because they do not conform to the Socratic ideals which are often assumed to enjoy a monopoly on virtue in Habermasian thought – an assumption which is neither entirely accurate nor comprehensively rebutted by Habermas himself. What it demands is an ongoing critical analysis of the cultural frames and the political economy of the mediascape; the diversity and inclusivity of media networks; and the disjunctures that prevail between our realistic aspirations for a mediascape that makes an increasingly complex world intelligible, more amenable to intervention, and open to new and unfamiliar ways of seeing, on the one hand, and 'actually existing' mediations, on the other.

A PUBLIC SPHERE IN BITS?

One suspects that Habermas is no e-mail junky, that he does not readily cut short the regular late-night discussions he convenes with colleagues and students in his favourite Greek restaurant in order to boot up and log on to a philsophically themed chat room or surf through the latest entries on his favourite blogs. His distaste for the online world can be glimpsed in a recent remark dismissing the Internet as a series of 'global villages'[36] that, far from contributing towards the emergence of a global public sphere, reflect and exacerbate the fragmentation of public life and the proliferation of cultural enclaves. Though we may want to dismiss this as irrational

Luddism, his scepticism may not be *entirely* misplaced. The hyped 1990s discourse of the 'digital revolution' (which, thankfully, has since been displaced if not replaced by some more sober assessments) was undergirded by at least two dominant rhetorics: sometimes one prevailed over the other, but sometimes they converged seamlessly. One of these was the rhetoric of neo-liberalism: the sovereign consumer would finally triumph in a mediascape characterised by abundance rather than scarcity and by the 'intelligent networks', responsive to the consumer's every whim, which were displacing the oppressive 'dumb terminals' of analogue mass media. The other dominant rhetorical device was an appeal to values which should surely tug at the Habermasian heart strings: the promise of radicalised citizenship (or 'netizenship') and a more participatory democracy. The two rhetorics would converge, most famously, in the funky-but-erudite pages of *Wired* magazine,[37] but also in the crusty old corridors of power.[38]

Probably the most pervasive keyword of this rhetorical landscape has been 'interactivity'. The point about digital technologies is that they are interactive: they allow us to talk back. What better news for advocates of the Habermasian public sphere than to be told that the era of mass, one-way communication flows is in terminal decline? Howard Rheingold declared the rise of 'electronic *agora*'.[39] Where the telephone facilitated one-to-one dialogue at a distance and the mass media worked on the monologic few-to-many 'broadcast' model, the new digital networks would transcend both the limitations and the 'anti-democratic' implications of analogue technologies. What the digiphiles announced was the arrival of unlimited bandwidth in which the roles of sender and receiver blur, in which we would be able to communicate with unprecedented freedom along both horizontal and vertical axes (citizen-to-citizen and citizen-to-institution). This would be the renaissance of dialogue, the advent of the 'electronic coffee house',[40] perhaps, in which citizens would (re)discover the art of speaking, debating, and discursively testing the claims of the powerful and of each other. Elitist or complacent mass-media industries would now have to fight to retain their aura of authority and expertise and would lose their power as gatekeepers of knowledge, culture and the public agenda. The very institutions that had once unleashed such revolutionary energies against the feudal powers had now themselves become twentieth-century fiefdoms that would in turn be unseated by the digital 'fifth estate'. As ordinary citizens became participants, rather than passive recipients, for only a modest capital outlay –

the cost of a PC and network connection – the flow of mediated communication could be uncoupled from commercial imperatives and the myriad listservs, blogging networks and discussion forums found on the Internet would privilege discussion for discussion's sake rather than for commercial gain or political leverage.

This is only partly a tongue-in-cheek caricature of 1990s digiphilia. I have certainly deleted several gigabytes of nuance and caveat. But the headlines remain the same. Optimism for the radical potential of new digital media has also permeated beyond the networks of vested interest and techno-boosterism and into the discourses of critical communications theory. Douglas Kellner, for example, whose work is strongly inflected by the eternal pessimists of the Frankfurt School, feels compelled to distinguish between the 'democratic technology' of the computer, conducive to a vibrant public sphere, and the 'passivity' of traditional broadcast media.[41] Mark Poster's post-structuralist framework leads him to dismiss the humanistic preoccupation with 'better' communication, in favour of investigating the new modes of 'subject constitution' afforded by the novel spaces, relations, practices and conventions of the digisphere.[42] But he, too, is moved by the ways in which hypertext and spatial navigation through digital media deprive traditional sources of authority of their canonical power and their ability to dictate the pathways we citizens beat through our texts.[43]

In reality, of course, the term 'interactivity' hides a multitude of sins.[44] The model that has been in the ascendancy is not, of course, the Habermasian café – though this lives on, not least in the phenomenal growth of web-log culture – but, rather, the digital hypermarket: proliferating menus, customisable information and entertainment services, and the rise of the 'me channel' are ostensibly extensions rather than a dethroning of the channel-hopping 'freedoms' already engendered by analogue broadcasting. Increasingly, digital communication networks are built asymmetrically, reserving more capacity for the download than the upload – a techno-cultural metonym that sits uneasily with the supposed flattening effect of digitisation. We have also witnessed the ongoing recuperation of the anarchic dynamics of digital culture. The proliferation of digital media has been accompanied by the rise of corporatised and methodologically opaque information guides (search engines, portals, 'smart' advertising tailored to individual profiles, commercially sponsored and carefully regulated online communities, and user-friendly interfaces) offering to guide the bewildered consumer–citizen through the blizzards of cultural and social detritus to the promised land of 'content' or of 'community' with like-minded others.

Of course, the problems of information overload in the digital mediascape are only the corollary of an obscure and complex society that is impossible to grasp in its totality. That is why, to reiterate a point made in the previous section, a key task for the democratic imagination is to think through how the expert systems of mediation on which we depend – even in the context of interactive and dialogic media – might become more accountable and diverse, and not simply be transcended. Even something so ostensibly unfettered by corporate logic as the Indymedia.org network of collaborative, alternative, grassroots news production provides a good case in point here. This is precisely the kind of institutional experiment that, on the one hand, challenges both the ideological frameworks *and* the methodologies and organisational structures of the dominant providers (such as CNN or BBC Online) yet, on the other hand, still demands both internal and external scrutiny of its editorial and organisational practices, its codes and conventions, precisely as it acquires the cachet of a major, alternative institution – a *system* – to which more and more citizens look for guidance and insight.

A second keyword for the digital age has been 'convergence', a promissory vision of telecommunications, computing and the cultural industries merging into a seamless web of information, entertainment and communication glued together by the universal language of binary digital code. All sorts of technical and economic obstacles have kept the dream (and, for some, the nightmare) of seamless convergence in the realm of 'vapourware'. Yet we have witnessed an unprecedented 'networking' of the mediascape with the rise of digital technologies, ranging from the hyperlinked synergies pursued by the cultural industries to the themed threads of the news sites and discussion forums: Dan Schiller has effectively shown how the digital mediascape can be read as the latest achievement of an always already 'hyperlinked' consumer culture that works to nudge citizens ceaselessly along commodity networks, motivating them with the knowledge (and inducing the anxiety) that there is always more and better to be had.[45] The dystopic take on digital convergence is that fulfilment of a Baudrillardian nightmare: the proliferation of fractured but self-sufficient simulacra in which, as consumer–citizens logged into our bespoke networks, ears plugged with headphones or glued to the cell phone, eyes trained on 'me screens' (whose function is, precisely, to *screen*), we find ourselves relieved of the requirement to intervene in a putative 'real world' that is no longer our ontological centre of gravity.[46]

The obvious response to this bleak prognosis would be to rattle off an impressive list of examples of citizens and activists using the Internet to intervene in that so-called 'real world' and, in doing so, fostering remarkably egalitarian – though rarely dispassionate or conflict-free – interactions. The distinction between the 'virtual' and the 'real' has been badly overplayed, most especially in pessimistic, rather than optimistic, discourses on digital culture: the digital pessimists would do well to spend a little more time online to acquaint themselves with some 'real world' examples! But rather than taking the standard option of trying to make a one-sided diagnosis look a little more balanced, I wish to take a slightly different turn here and raise the question of whether the increasing ubiquity, connectivity *and self-referential* nature of a digitised mediascape could actually be productive for our understanding of the Habermasian public sphere. Indeed, I want to suggest that there are two key ways in which the implications of this might be grasped differently as potentially positive moments in the transformation of the public sphere, whilst maintaining a critical eye for the dangers.

The first moment of positivity reflects back on something we discussed in Chapter 1: 'reflexive publicity' means applying the norms of critical publicity to the very institutions that are perceived to fulfil that role in respect of other institutions and power holders, not least the institutions of the media. The second moment is an outgrowth of the first and requires us to acknowledge the increasingly pervasive role that communications technologies play in struggles over the very 'fault-lines' – public–private and system–lifeworld, for example – which a Habermasian notion of politics emphasises.

Digital culture is precisely *not* just a mass of atomised cultural enclaves. The cultural industries may indeed invest a great deal of resources into profiling and niching consumers. We should also add that interest groups, subcultural communities and fandoms are often amenable to self-enclosure and exclusivity. But this has never been (and, I believe, will never be) the whole story. For a start, the profiling and niching processes characteristic of the digital age are increasingly automated through algorithms that are indifferent to questions of cultural atomism and increasingly hail consumers as nodes on a differential matrix rather than assigning them a categorical pigeon-hole, as mainstream market research in the cultural industries has previously tended to do. Internet cookies and Amazon.com (or TiVo) bespoke recommendations allow consumers to criss-cross all manner of counter-intuitive thresholds. They cater precisely for the gay, right-wing fan of Star Trek, soccer and Dogme movies. The point is not to uncritically celebrate this, for the menu may be eclectic but also depressingly safe, formulaic and superficial. The rise of an algorithmic surveillance culture may achieve new heights of reification: it may be more Weberian, systematised, depersonalised and opaque than anything that has gone before it. But the point is to acknowledge that even at the corporatised end of the spectrum, digital culture is woven from threads that can lead in suprising directions and does not necessarily engender an explosion of hermetically sealed 'sphericules'. Something more complex and contradictory is at stake.

With the rise of digital culture, we witness the emergence of many cultural forms and genres that, for want of a better phrase, leave threads hanging. Peter Lunenfeld has spoken of the 'culture of unfinish' that permeates the digital mediascape.[47] This is a useful way of grasping how digital media texts are almost always 'works in progress'. This is manifested in many different ways. In a simple sense, digital texts such as web sites, blogs, discussion forums and so on, admit of continual reworking and modification (and not just by an original 'author') in ways that were scarcely imaginable in the analogue era. Hypertext enthusiasts[48] have seen digital media as another nail in the coffin of the 'author', whose obituary had already been written by Roland Barthes.[49] This is an unnecessarily reductive and ethnographically remote formulation: the digital mediascape has of course multiplied the opportunities for citizens to partake in self-conscious 'authorship'; and it is also increasingly populated by digital texts (DVDs, time-based audio-visual media, etc.) that are not amenable to or intended for such reworking over time by the original producers, let alone by others. Digital culture does *not* signal the end of a cultural concern with authorship, control, intellectual property and textual boundaries; in problematising them, it has actually raised their profile. But even digital texts that embody notions of authorship and permanence frequently speak to the 'culture of unfinish': there are connections with other texts to be followed, there are different pathways through a text to experiment with, there are different environments and platforms to access the text through, there are comments to be posted, and so on. The most stark example from the point of view of our discussion might be an online news article on a particular issue that carries links to a government report cited in the article, a range of further related articles, and a discussion forum on the topic which, itself, carries more links to other destinations. But this example threatens to obscure the point, because it is not really the apparent 'communicative transparency' engendered by these encounters (such as the privilege of accessing 'primary' sources alongside their journalistic interpretations) that is most interesting here: in fact, we need to be deeply sceptical of the mythology of transparency which digital culture can seduce us with. Rather, what is most interesting is the prospect that the 'culture of unfinish' may, more broadly, help to foster a sense of being more at ease with the provisional, partial and decentred nature of our ways of viewing the world. Similarly, to respond that, on a macro scale, there exist high levels of circularity in evidence in the linking structures of the Internet and that there are many areas of the digital mediascape more generally that resemble walled gardens is really to miss the point. When an expanding and networked mediascape increasingly lays bare the limitations of our insights, we might experience anxieties and insecurities, responding fatalistically to the information blizzards we find ourselves caught up in ... *or* we might learn to better appreciate the provisional nature of our views such that we might become better listeners when we encounter difference and dissent. An appropriately provisional suggestion, then, is that digital culture *may* contribute to the enrichment of discourse ethics by foregrounding an 'ethic of unfinish'. A realistic assessment cautions strongly against the Deleuzian vision of the infinite concatenations of the digital 'rhizome'[50] that inspires many digital artists and activists. But where cultural pessimists see the digital mediascape comprising only cultural enclosures, an internal critique of the contradictions of digital culture reveals *at least the possibility* that it can militate *against* closure just as it promotes it.

This resonates most strongly with Habermas's notion of 'reflexive publicity' in *Structural Transformation*. The digital age may not equip us to see through the 'distortions' of mediated communication and unravel an objective (that is, unmediated) version of reality – in fact, it *multiplies* mediation. Indeed, as Jay David Bolter and Richard Grusin have argued,[51] we can always understand putatively 'new' communications technologies and media forms in terms of 'remediation'. In the drive for more 'authentic' modes of communication, new media forms invariably borrow and remix the codes and conventions for organising reality from preceding forms. But rather than simply conceiving these multiplying layers of mediation in terms of a tragic loss of the 'real', we can instead consider how they might productively contribute to a more discerning orientation towards mediation itself, one that acknowledges the inescapability of mediation but refuses to allow one form of mediation to have the last word – a sceptical spirit that recognises that the mediations of the public sphere, though they may resemble a 'second nature', might always be different. Multiple mediations may help us develop a heightened sensitivity to the partiality, the construction and the unfinished nature of mediated discourses. Cross-referencing against sources which construct radically different versions of reality can, of course, be productive; drifting through sources that share dominant frames but differ in shade and emphasis can still help to nudge us out of our default tendency to view things in black and white; even seeing the same chunk of text, image or sound pasted into different sources – digital culture is increasing modular, as Manovich[52] points out – may help attune us to the systemic constructions of mediated discourse. In this sense, we should perhaps radicalise the notion of reflexive publicity by seeing it as something not only demanded by the *institutions* of the public sphere, such as the media, but as something that should also be turned on ourselves as citizens. These are modest and tentative claims. Digital culture can surely engender cynics as well as reflexive sceptics; and it may even engender an arrogant rather than decentred cosmopolitanism, one that mistakes multiplicity for transcendent panopticism and communicative transparency. But the argument here is merely that we take seriously and critically interrogate digital culture, as we seek to investigate and deepen our understanding of the public sphere, not simply in terms of its capacity to inform or to misinform, to fragment or to unify, to engage or distract, but also at a deeper level in terms of the very constitution of citizenship and the different orientations citizens might take up in its midst.

Throughout this book, our encounter with the Habermasian politics of the public sphere has foregrounded a series of sociological and phenomenological 'fault-lines'. These fault-lines include: the public and the private; system and lifeworld; experts and citizens; anonymity and embodiment; the universal and the particular; the moral and the ethical; the global and the local; proximity and distance; presence and absence; the 'generalised other' and the 'concrete other'. I have tried to rescue these 'fault-lines' from becoming essentialist binaries, and I think this is a fair reflection of Habermas's own intentions, particularly in his later work. In any case, I hope I have at least shown how Habermasian theory unavoidably scratches at these fault-lines and brings them to the fore as important sites of contemporary political, cultural and theoretical tension and struggle.

Most discussions of the new mediascape and the public sphere have highlighted the role of, say, the Internet *as* a public sphere, focusing on how well or how poorly the practices it embodies live up to the values of Habermasian discourse ethics. But the problem here is that such enquiries highlight just part of the equation. They tend to treat the public sphere in abstraction from the broader socio-political and cultural context. I would like to suggest a complementary line of analysis that probes a little deeper and interrogates the mediascape *as* context and not merely as text, as foundation and not merely as edifice, as *langue* and not merely as *parole*. I take my cue for this from Habermas's own (albeit problematic) analysis, in *Structural Transformation* of the reconfiguration of (sub)urban spaces, the changing architectures of domestic space, the shifting nature of the culture industries and other related trends that underpinned the rise of 'privatism' and radically recontextualised the public sphere, its meanings and its locations. I take my cue also from Raymond Williams' contemporaneous work on 'mobile privatisation'[53] that implicated the television, the motor car and the rise of suburbia in fundamentally altered orientations towards the public world outside. By focusing on the rise of the digital mediascape (as opposed to, say, the rise of new urbanism), my comments risk betraying a media-centric world-view. This is not the intention. I want simply to suggest that rich analysis must try to rescue the mediascape from our rather one-dimensional and utilitarian urge to make it over in the image of the Habermasian public sphere by critically engaging its everyday and contextual aspects. My points here are meant to be forward-looking rather than summative: they offer just a few fragmented illustrations with the goal of stimulating further inquiry.

The mobile phone seems precisely to fit the bill of a profoundly quotidian technology and cultural form that has little to offer any analysis of the public sphere: the cellular networks are rarely alive with the sound of vigorous public debate (although there is nothing *essential* in the technology to make the development of new genres of cell-phone public discourse unimaginable). Yet, as something increasingly woven into the fabric of everyday existence in contemporary societies, the mobile phone, metonymically perhaps, raises important questions about the way we live and communicate in the world, which can be grasped at least partially in terms of a problematisation of 'public' and 'private'. An intuitive reading of the mobile phone might frame it in terms of an unprecedented rise of privatism and withdrawal from public space: if Raymond Williams saw the emergence of television engendering a culture that places value on 'going places' without having to physically travel, the mobile phone is in part a reverse reinforcer of 'mobile privatisation' in as much as it keeps us tied to the private sphere even as we physically traverse public spaces. An alternative formulation would be that mobile-phone culture signals just how meaningless the distinction between public and private has become: putatively private social relations burst forth into public space whilst the 'integrity' of the private realm is shattered by norms of social intercourse that require us to 'wear' mobiles like electronic tagging devices, keeping us accessible to the outside world 24/7. But an investigation that engaged the contradictions and tensions of mobile phone culture would interrogate the meaning of, say, the ongoing controversies over the 'etiquette' of using mobile phones in public places, and cross-cultural, gendered and inter-generational variations in use and practice,[54] asking how these things speak to the broader social and cultural context. Rather than making theoretical pronouncements, theoretically informed research should be asking more open questions: To what extent is the mobile phone helping to render the distinction between privacy and publicity culturally meaningless or phenomenologically hopeless? To what extent does it elicit defensive reactions that assert the 'sanctity' of private or public space? To what extent does it yield greater interest in or reflexivity in respect of the intersections of public and private (something that could possibly be conceived as a productive moment in the transformation of the public sphere)? The theoretical resources and research programmes to address these questions are still in their infancy. Indeed, the cultural consequences, themselves, in all their complexity, are only beginning to unfold.

George Myerson's book with the intriguing title *Heidegger, Habermas and the Mobile Phone*[55] sketches an interesting theoretical framework that could ignite some productive research, though his strategy misfires in one sense. Myerson implicates the mobile phone in the colonisation of the lifeworld thesis, arguing that mobile-phone culture privileges systemically coordinated communication over reciprocal, open-ended communication. I agree with Myerson that many of the dominant tropes of the culture are instrumental (we marvel at this new *tool* and wonder how we ever lived without it). Cost structures, miniaturisation, the elliptical codes of SMS text messaging and the like all speak to the values of communicative *economy*: the mobile is something we use to achieve a communicative goal in the most efficient way possible. Moreover, Myerson points out that although we still conceive of person-to-person communication as the core function of the mobile phone, corporations are continually devising new ways to constitute it as a tool for interaction between individuals and abstract systems or institutions: it threatens to become a technology of 'narrowcasting', a bespoke push-and-pull *provider* of information and entertainment services in the image of the 'me channel'.

But just as the telephone itself, since its nineteenth-century inception, has been a site of contest between competing models of communication (for example, the official discourses that promoted its instrumental and business uses versus the feminised discourses of chatter and 'keeping in touch', or historical examples of the telephone being used as a broadcasting system for news or music), so too the mobile phone is emerging as a yet more complex assemblage of contradictions, contestations and contingencies:[56] the cultural values of communicative economy in Finland, the birthplace of the mobile phone,[57] versus the tropes of connectivity and phatic communication that often accrue to it in other cultures (writing this in New Zealand, I am currently surrounded by advertisements for a new mobile phone service called 'Motormouth' whose tag line is simply 'blah, blah, blah, blah' – the 'system' restlessly strives to recuperate the inefficient and unruly lifeworld!); the uneven popularity of text messaging and picture messaging across the world; the relative failure, to date, of online information services (a pared down Internet in the hand), which are continually touted as the future for mobile phones: all these things suggest that the mobile phone may not be as amenable to 'systemic steering' as either the corporations *or* the cultural pessimists imagine. This is reinforced by a variety of subterranean affections for the mobile phone on the part of 'flash mobs', philanderers, football hooligans, criminal networks and so on. Moreover, I think we would benefit from more research on the way mobile phones and other communications devices are implicated in the *boundary disputes* between system and lifeworld and not merely in a narrative of colonisation which frames the lifeworld as mute victim.

How do we grasp the meaning of the digital citizen who trades the relative serendipities and collective frames of reference of the radio (one 'system') for the hyper-individualised abundance of the personal MP3 player (another 'system')? How do we read the student who sits through my lecture catching up on her text messages: clearly, I've made her bored, but can I also console myself with the thought that she may in some way be resisting the colonisation of her lifeworld by an opaque education 'system' that presents the canon of so many dead-white-European-male theorists as 'second nature'? How do we read the commuter standing at the train station, who dreams up calls she must make on her mobile in order to fend off the advances of a market researcher or street evangelist (whose perceived 'systematicity' is carved not out of an indifference to questions of value – quite the opposite – but out of an apparent extraterrestrial facticity that intrudes upon the commuter's lifeworld as if out of nowhere: she cannot see what they can possibly share in common).

On one level, these simplistic vignettes recall Rey Chow's resistive reading of the Chinese youth plugged into his Walkman: 'I am not there, not where you collect me.'[58] But we need to look beyond the binaries of resistance and incorporation. It may not be at all accurate to talk of 'resistance' when such devices are often implicated in processes of *configuring* those aspects of the system world (often in the guise of the culture industries) that are admitted into the lifeworld and those that are screened out. The 'system' is not a monolithic or internally coherent beast: my 'system world' (which includes the inescapable and pervasive facticity of mobile phones and their irritating incursions) is not identical with my student's (which includes, say, reams of paper detailing syllabi, course requirements and assessment criteria); the commuter's 'system world' (trains that run late or the daily hazards of street preachers and market researchers) is not identical with the 'system world' of the man selling religion at the train station (crowds so embroiled in the task of getting from A to B that they have forgotten to question what it's all about). Furthermore, we need to investigate the extent to which conceiving of these encounters as 'boundary disputes' actually resonates with the self-understandings of social actors themselves, and, again, the extent to which these encounters may gesture towards greater *reflexivity* (a citizenry better equipped to ask questions about the nature and scope of systemic logics), as opposed to the twin pitfalls of either an anti-systemic (anti-modern) reactionism or an uncritical embrace of the administered individualism on offer (both of which, it has to be said, seem to enjoy plenitude today).

My point is that we need to be critical and discriminatory in our investigations, but that theoretically informed research might help us to acquire both a deeper understanding of some of the cultural dynamics at stake in the ongoing development of intensively technologised social interactions, *and* a more nuanced conceptual framework that acknowledges the tensions between public and private, system and lifeworld and so forth, in terms of complex *boundary disputes* that are subject to ongoing *mediation* and do not necessarily admit of interpretive *or* ontological closure. To that extent, our concern with 'mediation' has moved beyond the either/or purview of intersubjectivity versus money and power, to acknowledge the array of technologies and cultural forms that intervene and are taken up as weapons (by all sides) in these ongoing disputes. My biased emphasis on the public–private and system–lifeworld fault-lines, not to mention my perverse fascination with the mobile phone, is not intended to obscure the many other lines of inquiry that vie for our attention. For example, we know that Internet chat rooms, listservs and virtual communities are littered with boundary disputes involving anonymity and embodiment, experts and non-experts, the local and global, to name a few. There is much existing and ongoing research that demonstrates how pervasive these boundary disputes are. The Internet has, for instance, played to dreams of a zone where 'I can really be me' or, at least, where 'I can explore and experiment with various narratives of me'[59] free from the prohibitions and inhibitions of face-to-face encounters – the 'Other' can be generalised so that I can truly be 'concrete'. It's also a zone where dreams of authorship and 'audience-oriented subjectivity' can run amok – the imagined audience and the delusions of transcendence or disembodiment afforded by the Internet paints *Homo digitalis* as something akin to Gutenberg Man on steroids. And yet, because so much of what goes on in these forums falls between the poles of the face-to-face community and the generalised other of the broadcast model, all sorts of conflicts ensue as possibilities for abuse and power games multiply under the shroud of anonymity. To outsiders, the tensions around online 'flaming', 'trolling', gender-bending and identity play may look like nerdish trivia, and yet they are rich case studies in conflicts surrounding the ethics of the 'Other' which are instructive for our understanding of the public sphere and its cultural context.

The proliferation of online pornography provides a useful counter to what may sound like a dangerously sanguine take on the potential for digital culture to stimulate greater reflexivity in respect of these boundary disputes. If (gendered) dreams of transcendence and disembodiment flow abundantly through the Internet,[60] so too do *bodies*. It has been (plausibly) suggested that the Internet affords a certain decommodification or reclamation of the female body that may enable some women to control the terms on which their bodies are disseminated, something which sets it apart from traditional and more exploitative outlets. At the same time, the way in which online culture rips symbols more comprehensively from their points of origin than Walter Benjamin[61] could ever have imagined, makes the provenance of pornographic images (and the monetary or exploitative relations that may have shaped their production) extremely opaque, whilst the anonymity and instantaneous mode of its (predominantly male) reception helps to smooth out any anxieties that consumers may have about them in this regard. That digital culture can blur boundaries and *deter* reflexivity is not in question, then. My point is that the contradictions and complexities of digital culture must be taken seriously if we are to deepen our understanding of the public sphere and the culture of reflexivity to which a Habermasian discourse ethics necessarily appeals.

My aim in this chapter has simply been to scratch a little at the problem of mediation. If it is to be truly relevant to our world today, the theory of the public sphere must not content itself with being a theory of communication: it must also become a theory of *mediation*, which is not in fact the same thing. Our analysis of mediation must look beyond the role of the media as a conduit for ideas, symbols and messages, and beyond the 'media' of power and money: it must also engage with the mediation of those cultural fault-lines and boundaries that shape both the fissures of contemporary society *and* our aspirations for a better one. To pre-empt the moral of the next and final chapter: there is not merely unfinished business, but important and complex business that has scarcely begun.

5
Unfinished Projects:
Reflexive Democracy

In the course of this discussion, and particularly in the previous chapter, it has become clear that, to a significant degree, the Habermasian idea of the public sphere hangs on the question of *reflexivity*. The concept of the public sphere becomes most productive when it is considered within the context of a culture of reflexivity. It is this culture of reflexivity that energises the public sphere, problematising once unquestioned values and institutions and leading to demands for new ways of managing contradiction, conflict and difference. And in the Habermasian model, the public sphere and its reflexive context must be mutually reinforcing: the public sphere takes on the role of a kind of exemplary space for the considered, deliberative and, as far as possible, egalitarian weighing of competing claims, an ethic that can at least rub off on – though by no means colonise – the more unruly and visceral micro-practices and discourses of everyday life. We have also seen how this culture of reflexivity is not simplistically inscribed in historically unfolding competencies, though this implication may be gleaned from an isolated reading of Habermas's mid-career writings: in *The Theory of Communicative Action* and related works, Habermas places perhaps excessive store by the emergence of 'post-conventional' capacities which render modern human agents better placed than their pre-modern counterparts to historicise, that is, to contextualise and criticise their own historical situations and individual biographies. In his early work on the public sphere, Habermas more successfully highlighted the historical contingencies of specific institutions and modern 'traditions' (including concrete constitutional and journalistic cultures) which must form the backdrop to any analysis of cultural reflexivity. In his more recent work, Habermas places greater store by another layer of 'contingency': the rise of an ethical orientation that self-consciously *affirms* a reflexive attitude towards our subjective, intersubjective and institutional structures in the context of communicative relations judged according to standards of openness and reciprocity. But throughout these modulations in Habermas's broader philosophy of history, the question of reflexivity has been central to his entire intellectual project.

Habermas has summarised the general orientation of his work in terms of the 'unfinished project of modernity'. In drawing our discussion to a close, I want to suggest that we consider the unfinished project to be, instead, one of 'reflexive modernity'. This is not my neologism, of course: I want to stage an encounter here between the Habermasian politics of the public sphere and the discourse of reflexive modernity that has, under the auspices of Ulrich Beck and Anthony Giddens in particular, cast its influence over the sociological imaginary during the past decade or so. In doing so, I am holding true to the tactic that I outlined in the introduction: by staging encounters with thinkers whose disputes with Habermas could be described as internal (though by no means trivial), I hope to arrive at a close reading and rich sense of the merits and pitfalls of the Habermasian project. This is a tactic that can complement, rather than trump, the more common one of analysing the great theory wars separating Habermas from his philosophical arch-rivals.

Beck has argued that 'reflexive modernity' demands the 'reinvention of politics'.[1] I suggest that this impulse is broadly in keeping with the Habermasian project, despite the conservatism we may be tempted to read into Habermas's recent focus on constitutional patriotism (Chapter 3). Or, to put it another way, I suggest that the Habermasian narrative of the public sphere teaches us that, whether we like it or not (and, indeed, whether Habermas himself likes it or not), the very meanings that we attach to the words 'politics', 'citizenship' and 'democracy' are (and must be) up for grabs even as we seek to defend them. What's called for is a process of continual reinvention and renewal. We cannot rely on God, Nature or Reason to run to our rescue and take this task off our hands or, rather, in our pluralistic times, we cannot allow any one specific version of God, Nature or Reason to prevail at the expense of another. But *because* we cannot 'reinvent' *ex nihilo*, then our own particular gods (and demons), our own reasons, and our own versions of 'nature' (both human and non-human) – our lifeworlds in all their diversity – provide simultaneously the raw material of *and* the greatest challenge to the new politics. It's important to emphasise that, if the term 'reinvention' is appropriate at all, it cannot signify anything like a clean break with the past. Indeed, the shifting political sands identified in the discourse of reflexive modernity can be traced back at least as far as the emergence of late capitalism itself. What's more, I shall want to conclude by suggesting that Habermas ultimately offers a persuasive argument for the ongoing relevance of certain values which, at their most abstract, have been coterminous with the Enlightenment project itself.

The 'new' politics of reflexive modernity, then, bubble up to the surface in the context of opaque and shifting power relations which increasingly escape the grasp of liberal democracy's official polity. The welfare state once promised to empower its citizens through a range of de facto rights. It promised to protect them against the extremities of an untamed market and it promised to redistribute the fruits of economic growth according to principles of justice. Now, acute scepticism (or cynicism) towards these ideals informs the contemporary Zeitgeist. Radical 'Leftist' politics have lost their way. The goal of full employment has long been in its death throes. Ambitious national and even regional protectionist policies have been unimpressive in the face of global capital's immense mobility and power of veto. The inequalities between rich and poor have widened to scandalous proportions both internationally and within national societies. Fiscal crisis is routinely acknowledged as an endemic feature of the welfare state. The old Keynesian model of economic growth and full employment certainly offers no answers of its own to the ecological damage that it unleashed and which has since accelerated, unchecked, under the auspices of both neo-liberal and 'Third Way' social-democracy experiments.[2] And the politicisation of the private sphere has seemingly turned out to equal something other than the *democratisation* of everyday life: this is highlighted by the apparently contradictory phenomena of periodic popular backlashes against a 'nanny state' which is perceived as a remote and unwelcome force seeking to micro-manage aspects of everyday life such as child rearing, employment practices and school curricula, and, on the other hand, ongoing campaigns required to address domestic violence, children's rights, income disparities between genders and so forth. In sum, these depressing realities may be largely responsible for a political vacuum on the Left; but they are also stimulating new ways of conceiving progressive politics.

REFLEXIVE AGENCY

As we have seen, one way to begin mapping the new modes of struggle and conflict within this context is to consider the different 'fault-lines' along which they seem to be emerging. But what, briefly, of the 'old' fault-lines of the 'old' politics? It is important to recognise that two of the most fundamental fault-lines of the 'old' politics of modernity – capital–labour relations and the public–private dichotomy (manifested especially in conflicts over the welfare state, family law and issues of gender equality) – both seem unlikely to disappear from view. They have, however, been decentred and must now compete for attention with other fault-lines.

What, then, of the 'new' fault-lines? Giddens offers us a way in to this. The official polity is increasingly ill equipped to mediate the power relations of contemporary life because it remains territorially anchored and localised, whilst social interactions and connections are continuously and increasingly 'deterritorialised'. Communications media, transportation, migration, the mobility of financial capital, the global scope of ecological problems and biomedical hazards: all highlight the limitations of social democratic (not to mention Marxist) models of the cybernetic society where the state functions as a political nerve centre. The ascendant model is one based instead upon a network of 'flows' in which the state must shed its omniscient pretensions and adopt an increasingly reactive and disciplined orientation towards crisis avoidance – this is the end of the dream (or nightmare) of 'organised capitalism', in other words. 'The revolutionary changes of our time', Giddens claims, 'are not happening so much in the orthodox political domain as along the fault-lines of the interaction of local and global transformations.'[3] 'Action at a distance' becomes routine as the increasing elasticity of social relations stretched across space and time helps to foster an awareness that local events can be globally consequential, and vice versa. The Green cliché 'Think global; act local' attributes a political significance to that awareness. But what Giddens claims is that globalisation is not something that merely extends or stretches social relations; it also has ramifications for the individual at the deepest levels of consciousness and self-awareness. It paves the way for a reconfigured selfhood that is more attuned to complexity: utopias, blueprints and fatalistic religious narratives are treated with increasing disdain, something that Lyotard famously captured as the 'incredulity towards metanarratives' characteristic of the postmodern condition.[4] But, in contrast to the nihilistic drift of most postmodern discourse, Giddens also sees this reconfigured selfhood as one that is more attuned to the task of making the best possible decisions in a context of 'radical uncertainty'.

The intrusion of abstract systems into the fabric of everyday existence calls not for a politics of resistance, Giddens argues (although he recognises that such reactions are increasingly prevalent), but for a politics of engagement. Nobody, even (or especially) within the most mundane of life situations, can avoid the influence of abstract systems: every time we eat, take a pill, drive a car, visit an ATM, board a plane or turn on a light, we enter into a Faustian pact with the institutions that empower us to go about our lives whilst making us staggeringly dependent upon opaque systems and absent others.[5] There is also a heightened awareness that these abstract systems, many of which serve to *protect* us from biomedical, economic and other sorts of hazard, also *generate* a plethora of their own, manufactured risks. A politics of engagement, in Giddens' scheme of things, is one which works along the axis of *risk* and *trust*. We live in an era of unprecedented scepticism *and* dependency in which issues of what Giddens calls 'ontological security' come to the fore. These issues can be addressed only through engagement: at best, they may only be temporarily repressed when we adopt an attitude of pragmatic fatalism.[6] By 'engagement', Giddens does not simply mean that the new politics must strive to make expert systems more transparent and democratically accountable. A politics of engagement is not geared towards the eradication of uncertainty and absence but, rather, the generation of 'active trust'. Using Erving Goffman's distinction between the 'frontstage' and 'backstage' operations of institutions, Giddens remarks:

> Although everyone is aware that the real repository of trust is in the abstract system, rather than the individuals who in specific contexts 'represent it', access points carry a reminder that it is flesh-and-blood people (who are potentially fallible) who are its operators.[7]

Absent relations, or 'faceless commitments' as he calls them, must be re-embedded in the context of personalised 'facework':[8] institutions must 'front up', so to speak. But this is not the same thing as requiring institutions to turn themselves inside out for the purposes of unrestricted public scrutiny. The distinction between 'frontstage' and 'backstage', rather than disappearing, becomes a more fluid zone of contention. The contemporary world may be populated by human agents that are, by default, willing to grant powerful institutions their autonomy: most of us lead busy lives and, left to their own devices, those institutions are often critical for our ability to manage those busy lives. But the contemporary world is also populated by increasingly savvy citizens who are capable of making institutions vulnerable whenever they fail to front up over contentious issues, by withholding information, misleading, or refusing to answer questions. Citizens, when suitably motivated, are increasingly proficient at prising open institutions and breaching the official boundaries between frontstage and backstage. We live, Giddens touchingly reminds us, in a 'world of clever people'![9]

But the rising stock of 'expert' knowledge that 'lay' citizens are capable of acquiring through education, the Internet and self-help literature, say, is only part of the equation. For example, institutionalised scepticism and professional competition routinely lead to open conflicts ensuing *between* and *within* expert systems: large industries and professions are rarely monolithic forces that speak with a single voice. Intractable arguments frequently go on in public over how to *interpret* a statistical 'fact' (economic 'data' is especially adept at generating more questions than answers). The media often make it their business to try to tear away the veils of autonomy worn by scientific or political institutions (and often rival media institutions) by exposing their links with special-interest groups and corporations. And crucially, there is growing public attention given to 'manufactured' hazards: powerful techno-scientific institutions are 'always already' implicated in a web of problems and remedies – though perhaps not subject to the same levels of public cynicism as most political institutions, they are also largely unable to command unconditional trust and must invest heavily in ongoing proactive and reactive public relations. All of this systemic entropy may have little to do with increased *transparency*. It may ultimately succeed in generating greater uncertainty and confusion among lay citizens ('the more we find out, the less we know'). But it also undermines the traditional aura of expertise and unquestioned faith to which expert institutions may have once aspired: citizens are increasingly moved to get their hands dirty and to dig for answers themselves, even where they remain dependent on expert systems in the last analysis. Consider, for example, the medical patient who turns to the Internet in frustration at her doctor's inability to make a firm diagnosis. Her reflexive agency does not reduce her ultimate dependency on the medical profession. Having found some relevant information on the Internet, which itself has been provided by medical experts, she will then have to persuade the relevant specialists to re-evaluate her case in the light of that information. In the event that she overcomes that hurdle, she will then depend on expert professionals to provide her with the appropriate treatment. In this scenario, in other words, experts are decentred and multiplied, but in no sense is the expert system transcended or downgraded in importance. Rather, in this ascendant culture of reflexivity, when expert claims enter the universe of lay discourse, they must increasingly compete with other expert claims and engage with the reflexive capacities of lay agents themselves.[10]

The world in which we live is, apparently, one of increased scepticism, knowledgeability and reflexivity. Giddens' new politics seeks new ways of engaging with, rather than unrealistically eliminating or withdrawing from, the opportunities and risks of modernity. Social actors (both citizens and institutions) are condemned to make choices whose consequences cannot be predicted with absolute certainty, not least because inaction or withdrawal carries (often intolerable) risks of its own (consider, for example, the dilemmas that vaccination programmes pose for parents, or the social disabilities that follow from a decision to avoid the considerable dangers of car travel). Whether we opt for the swings or the roundabouts, the new reflexive modernity offers us neither the certitude of 'providential reason' once promised by the Enlightenment, nor the nostalgic path back to Mother Nature implicated in many ecological discourses.[11]

Giddens' model of reflexive agency may be a useful one. Despite its rather pragmatic, anti-utopianism (Giddens argues that we must abandon 'emancipatory politics' in favour of 'life politics'), it is, on one level, a rather sanguine reading of late modernity. But there is also a missing dimension that I think actually renders it a rather bleak narrative. His portrait of reflexive modernity is ultimately rather solipsistic. He depicts a world of individuals who deploy their reflexive capacities to negotiate their relations with others and with expert systems. But the intersubjective dimension – the question of how we deal with each other *as subjects* – is largely absent. Granted, Giddens argues that we need more *dialogue* between individuals and between citizens and institutions. But there is nothing that raises dialogue above its default status as a conduit along which the mute 'data' of information, insight, views and experiences can flow. Dialogue functions rather like a bridge on which we can agree to meet in compromise before scurrying back to our own lifeworlds: the real reflexive action takes place on the terra firma of the 'clever' individual. We get little insight into the intractable problems of discussing how 'we' might want to live together in moral communities and how 'we', under whichever voluntary or ascriptive markers of collective identity (as a group, as a 'society', as a species, perhaps), might try to steer expert systems in a particular direction. The centre of gravity is the individual who, left to his own devices by the flight of collective certitudes once gifted by religion, by nationalism, or by traditional communities, must bear ultimate responsibility for his actions. We get little sense of the scale of the battle between expert systems and lay citizens – a scale that *demands* collective responses – when the increasing reflexivity of citizens is met with a huge scaling up of those 'frontstage' operations, namely sophisticated and obfuscatory public relations. We get little insight into the intersubjective contexts in which 'individualisation' develops and the actual and potential role that *public* contexts, shaped by difference and conflict, might play. We get little purchase on the question of 'cultural membership' and the 'inclusion' of diverse individuals and subcultural groups within the collective frameworks, such as the nation, that speak and act on their behalf: Habermas still refers to this as the problem of 'solidarity', though as recent discourse has highlighted, it might be usefully reframed as 'cultural citizenship'.[12] My point is not that Giddens himself is unaware of debates about deliberative democracy, about the discursive constitution of identity, or about the questions of solidarity and cultural citizenship. But he focuses firmly on the task of rescuing self-help groups or the prevalent focus on self-identity, health and diet, from blanket condemnation by those who would see this apparent preoccupation with the 'self' as symptomatic of a pathetic narcissism or privatistic withdrawal: Giddens, by contrast, wants us to read this focus on the 'self' as a positive sign of increasingly reflexive agency.[13] This is not an intrinsically bad aim (though we should also avoid sliding into a celebratory account of self-help groups and the politics of self-identity). But what is important is that we still lack a narrative of reflexive modernity that foregrounds the intractable problems of the first person *plural*.

Giddens' 'life politics' gesture beyond the limited horizon of consumer 'politics' in substance but fail to do so in form. The collective action sites of self-help, voluntary and single-issue groups are conceived less as vehicles for the radical democratisation of expert systems and more as symbols of an ascendant culture of reflexivity responsible for eroding institutional conceit. *Too much* democratisation would conflict with the conservative bias which Scott Lash and John Urry have correctly detected in Giddens' overriding concern with the concept of 'ontological security',[14] which foregrounds the psychological need for stability and order. What matters is that the relationship between expert systems and lay actors has been or is being radically transformed for the better in a *qualitative* sense. The pathologies of late modernity, it seems, revolve around the uneven distribution of chances for self-realisation which systems provide. In late modernity, the anxieties brought about by detraditionalisation and manufactured risk are not the exclusive preserve of the affluent. If the search for meaning and a place in the world is hindered but never cancelled out by material scarcity, then the question must be one of how to incorporate those who suffer from the double deprivation of material and symbolic resources into the reflexive fold.[15] Despite its individualistic thrust, Giddens' reflexive modernity is in one sense haunted more by Marx than by Weber: the pathologies of late modernity stem not from having taken a wrong turn down a particular path of rationalisation but, instead, from not having travelled far enough down it.

RISK AND REFLEXIVITY

Ulrich Beck's account of the 'risk society'[16] is certainly a darker one, but it also entertains a dash of optimism about prospects for more radical change. For a start, there is a slightly different emphasis. Whilst Beck sees the increased intensity of issues surrounding self-identity, work and leisure as integral to reflexive modernity, he is, first and foremost, an ecologist horrified by problems that threaten no less than the survival of the planet and its life forms. In the face of manufactured risk and the closed door on a return to nature, Beck paints rather less in the way of swings and roundabouts and rather more in the way of devils and deep blue seas.

Where the key conflicts underpinning industrial society have been ones concerned with the distribution of 'goods', we are moving under the auspices of the risk society, in Beck's account at least, towards a situation in which more and more key conflicts emerge around the distribution of 'bads': the distribution of environmental, economic and psychological risks. The 'risk society' is a novel formation not because the prevalence of risks is a new phenomenon or because we live in 'riskier times', but because the characteristics of risk are different from those of previous eras. Today's key risks implicate human institutions to an unprecedented degree: even where risks are not manufactured, as such, we perceive human institutions to be contributing to 'natural' risks when they fail to define or predict them adequately – consider the critical questioning faced by seismologists in the aftermath of the Asian Boxing Day tsunami. Moreover, risks are increasingly mobile and travel widely from their places of origin (British pollution causes acid rainfall in Scandinavia, economic decisions made on one side of the globe create unemployment on the other, and so on). And risks seem increasingly complex and difficult to define or calculate *before* the fact and before irreversible consequences have appeared. Fears around genetic modification or the impact of our increased reliance on antibiotics upon the immune systems of future generations, for example, are based on largely incalculable risks.[17] Risks must be anticipated increasingly through thought experiments, computer assisted modelling and hypothetical scenarios: scientific inquiry becomes, of necessity, increasingly *counterfactual*. The risks involved in a new medical procedure become rapidly apparent when fifty out of a hundred patients die on the operating table. That kind of 'simple' risk assessment is unproblematic (except for those unfortunate 'statistics'). Empiricism does not serve us well, on the other hand, when it comes to profiling the long-term consequences of genetic modification, just as an individual could hardly wait and see how long he lives before he decides whether to change his diet. Increasingly, risk profiles have to be discursively constructed, or 'scientifically born', as Beck puts it.[18] The conflicts that emerge over the definitions of risk and the symbolic castings of imagined futures are increasingly politicised and taken up in public discourse,[19] as the competing narratives of genetic modification have highlighted in recent years: the virtues of scientific 'progress' and the potential elimination of hunger versus the dangers of 'Frankenstein foods'.

Thus far, Beck's 'risk society' fits with Giddens's reflexive modernity. Both emphasise the blurring of distinction between risk *definition* and risk *creation* (all expert systems and, ultimately, all citizens, are implicated in *both*). Modernity's mythological uncoupling of 'nature' and 'society' becomes increasingly untenable as institutional knowledge and its application feed back into the very risk profiles they address, and as our relations with 'nature' (the sphere of 'facticity' in its broadest sense) become inextricably bound up in our relations with *each other* as we struggle over the definition and distribution of nature's 'goods' and 'bads'. But where Giddens' reflexive modernity focuses predominantly on the intersections between individual and expert system, Beck's analysis proves better equipped to address one of the most vexing problems of our time: the paradox of institutionalised hyper-specialisation and late modernity's cultural *de*-differentiation of 'value spheres' (after Weber) – science, law and morality, and aesthetics. The obscurity of the problems we face stems not only from incalculability and the inability to isolate facts. It also stems from the fact that the veil of autonomy has been lifted from the production of natural and social scientific knowledge. This is not simply because of the political and commercial interests that fund and shape it (something we might wishfully conceive as a *distortion* that could be ironed out), but also because science is always already implicated in political struggles to define and symbolically construct 'nature' and its trajectories.

So whilst the moral, ethical and aesthetic questions which are thrown up by genetic engineering or urban planning, say, take on increased urgency, we lack democratic institutions that can facilitate debate *across* the disciplines, that is, across Weber's value spheres, as well as between citizens and specific institutions. The media perform this intermediary function with varying degrees of credibility, but the idea that such a function should be the exclusive preserve of professional media institutions is deeply problematic. The media obey specific logics governed by both convention and structural constraint, and, in the main, are exempt from any *formal* responsibility to ensure fair, open and representative discourse (beyond a set of minimal negative prohibitions). And they lack any *formal* power (or 'right') to have their deliberations taken account of in upper levels of political representation. The media are *not* formally governed by the principles of either justice or sovereignty, and this underscores both their democratic importance and their democratic impotence.

Reflexive modernity, in Beck's account, demands an enhanced 'separation of powers' and a diversification of both formal and informal institutions of debate driven by the challenges of de-differentiation. Expert systems, including scientific institutions, are unavoidably reflexive insofar as they must increasingly address the consequences of their actions – they become source, definer and remedy *simultaneously*. It's clear, for example, that economic growth is driven increasingly by its own destructive side effects: drugs to treat burgeoning allergies, therapies to treat stress, green consumer goods to help us do our bit, an environmental clean-up industry (especially busy after military conflicts), tourism which feeds on the need to 'get away from it all', an insurance industry that thrives on the proliferation of risk, and so on. But to call this 'reflexivity' in an objective sense, as Beck makes clear, is not the same thing as a *culture of reflexivity*: it actually underscores the *lack* of enlightened and interdisciplinary reflection that engages scientific, moral and aesthetic questions, that empowers citizens to exert more influence, or that forces expert systems to critically reflect (rather than simply to capitalise) upon their own externalities.[20] The unimpeded 'logic of technique' remains, as Zygmunt Bauman puts it, a logic of fragmentation – the market must artificially isolate and privatise risks and remedies.[21] And where risks don't create calculable market opportunities to attract consumers or voters, then intransigence prevails, justified by the absence of that fictive commodity, absolute proof.[22] Where expert systems do promote an internal scepticism, the tendency will still be to present knowledge externally with apparent certitude,[23] and to intensively police those frontstage–backstage boundaries. And as the ideal of disinterested knowledge disappears from view and the public are confronted with a blizzard of competing assertions, Beck decries a 'feudalisation' of expert knowledge[24] which makes it impossible to discriminate between the integrity and validity of claims offered by the various interest groups, be they governments, corporations, the medical profession, the Food Commission, consumer groups, trade unions and so forth. Such a climate breeds increasing *cynicism*, and not merely scepticism, towards expert knowledge itself. Expert knowledge looks increasingly like a made-to-order commodity, generated for and sold to those interest groups that can afford to fund research.[25] Beck's reflexive modernisation, then, proceeds in an erratic, nature-like and most unreflective fashion.

A scandalised Beck nevertheless advances some ambitious remedial proposals. The answer is not simply more centralised state control over science and business. Such thinking falls prey to the cybernetic fallacy and, in reality, would create new bottlenecks through which the scope of debate and channels of problem definition, so desperately in need of broadening, would be further strangled by the 'economic Cyclopia of techno-scientific rationality'.[26] What's required, in fact, is a radical decentralisation of powers that would enable citizens to become more involved in the management of their local environments. But the globalisation and deterritorialisation of risks also mean that new institutions need to be imagined at global, regional and national levels. Beck argues for the concept of an 'ecological upper house', for example, which would include representatives of science, politics, the legal profession, citizen and consumer groups, trade unions and so forth. But such institutions would exist to convene and to mediate the broader range of discourses and debates that go on below, in the realm of 'sub-politics', and not to substitute for them. The point is not to undermine the autonomy of diverse sub-political discourses which go on in the professions, social movements, trade unions, protest groups, subcultural groups and business, nor is it to undermine the specialisation of expert knowledge. Rather, the point is to *radicalise* the idea of a 'separation of powers' and a decentred, differential politics,[27] facilitating more dialogue and instituting fair negotiation *across* the various sub-political arenas. Beck's politics of reflexive modernity aspires to enrich 'specialisation in the context',[28] and to empower sub-political groupings such as protest movements, trade unions and the like.[29]

Beck's notion of 'sub-politics' is especially important here because it immediately connects with dilemmas of the public sphere which have raised themselves in different ways throughout this study. It speaks to Nancy Fraser's claim that any model of radical democracy must accommodate both official and subaltern public spheres (Chapter 1), and it speaks to Habermas's colonisation of the lifeworld thesis (Chapter 3). Beck's model of sub-politics is driven by his desire to see significant interest groups of every hue brought into the formal political process. Today, there are special-interest groups that benefit greatly from lobbying and interacting with political representatives away from the gaze of publicity. Others, including pressure groups, can be disadvantaged by this separation of political form and content as they are forced to plough scarce resources into tactical battles for visibility. Bringing interest groups into the purview of a restructured formal democracy, premised on a greater separation of powers, would enhance both the accountability *and* the enfranchisement of the various interest groups and public spheres. But this sub-political model, if it is to be of value to the democratic imagination, must also be attuned to the dangers of co-option. In order to protect the autonomy and integrity of sub-politics, in all its diversity, the formal democratic process would not only need to find ways of ensuring that the agenda is set bottom-up, rather than top-down. It would also need to find ways of cultivating, respecting and drawing upon diverse *ways of doing things*: codes, conventions, rules, rituals and traditions. In our discussion of constitutional patriotism (Chapter 3), we noted that procedural common ground – the *constitution*, in the broadest sense – could be conceived as potentially cross-cultural only insofar as it is built and renewed in the light of diverse cultural *specificities*: it must aspire towards the *translocal*, rather than the global, in other words. We must also take seriously the dangers of simply multiplying strategic opportunism through a vertical and horizontal separation of powers: why would sub-political groups favour a communicative and cooperative orientation when finally granted the official voice that they have hitherto been denied? In acknowledging this danger, the very concept of sub-politics must be reflexively opened up. A settled definition of 'sub-politics' imperils the prefix that signifies its alterity. Rather than picturing sub-politics as a particular nexus of institutions, a radicalised model of democracy must be on the lookout for new and unpredictable sites of sub-politics and new modes of *being political*, even as it looks for ways of enfranchising and formally incorporating the visible sub-politics of the present. As we know from existing political cultures, today's sub-politics can so easily congeal into tomorrow's systemic 'nature'.

REVISITING THE PUBLIC SPHERE

For Habermas, of course, the fault-line between system and lifeworld is precisely the context for much of the new sub-politics. At the centre of Habermas's critical theory is a belief that, in the transition from tradition to modernity, capitalist development has engendered a one-sided form of rationalisation, one that privileges systemic imperatives. The result is that the lifeworld loses its capacity to shape an increasingly autonomous system and the discourses of means and ends pass like ships in the night. But, moreover, the reflexivity of the post-traditional lifeworld harbours an emancipatory potential which is squandered by the path of capitalist modernisation that we have been following. The administrative tentacles of the welfare state have intruded into the fabric of everyday life; political debate has become scientifically managed; capitalism has learned to commodify and instrumentalise education, sexuality, death, leisure, tourism, artistic endeavour, and the myriad other sites of cultural practice implicated in contemporary struggles for meaning. The path from tradition to modernity has not yet, at least, turned out to be one of emancipation from reified social structures.

Giddens has given the Habermasian grand narrative short shrift. He finds deeply problematic the notion that communicative action functions as a missing third term in a world caught between tradition and 'system'. But his disdain for the counterfactual ideals of Habermasian discourse ethics is also problematic. On the one hand, Giddens celebrates the ideals of 'dialogic democracy' but uses this term to encompass everything from active trust in abstract systems to the so-called 'pure relationship' of the intimate sphere. On the other hand, it's not clear how someone who values dialogue can avoid making implicit reference to an ideal or 'counterfactual' ethic. Giddens describes fundamentalism, for example, as 'refusal of dialogue'.[30] We might venture, then, that the widespread institutional inertia of consumer capitalism also qualifies as a kind of systemic fundamentalism, on this definition. But religious and political fundamentalisms, at least, are rarely silent. They speak their name loudly through television, the Internet and whatever channels are available. Noise – and not dialogue – is the opposite of silence. Even if we embrace 'noise' as an inescapable and potentially liberating aspect of all communication (and it can be), the limit case of fundamentalism shows, as if it were necessary, that an ethics of dialogue must be a discriminatory one: it can't shake off the aspirational norms of reciprocity and openness when it confronts the manifold shortcomings of real-life communications.

Conservative sub-politics doesn't, of course, enjoy a monopoly on fundamentalist tendencies and anti-democratic methods. Ostensibly progressive elements of sub-politics, both red and green in hue, frequently lack, or lose, even the aspirations of egalitarian and inclusive participation, or open and frank communication. Perhaps this is what ultimately links the earnest values of the grass-roots activist, the anti-racism campaigner, the anti-immigration campaigner, the self-help group, the local neighbourhood watch group, and even the 'keep our village tidy' campaigner with the postmodern tribes of identity politics, fandom, style cliques, flash mobs and bloggers who range across the touchstones of self-identity, irony, camp and the carnivalesque in preference over the pretensions of 'old fashioned' politicking. In most cases they are linked by a desire to liberate cultural praxis from the rigid parameters of consumer capitalism and the welfare state; they all express antipathy towards systemic fundamentalism, even where they generate alternative lifeworld fundamentalisms of their own.

This may be a needle of connection in a haystack of difference. What it does, though, is to underscore how the tensions between system and lifeworld cut across radically different sites of practice that may not only be ideologically incommensurable, but which can also entertain radically different notions of what 'politics' actually means: to the earnest activists, for example, the concerns of the postmodern tribes look frivolous and apolitical; to the postmodern tribes, the earnest activists remain stubbornly wedded to a politics of resistance against top-down power which is both futile and blind to the fertile micro-politics of everyday life. Of course, I have overdramatised this distinction in order to make more of the connection: in reality these 'postmodern' and 'earnest' orientations are not mutually exclusive and often inform groups or individuals simultaneously. The real point, however, is that the tension between system and lifeworld speaks to the *necessary reflexivity of sub-politics*. If we follow Habermas's theory of system and lifeworld to its conclusion, we see that it doesn't simply alert us to the dangers of bracketing off questions of political culture, but that it embodies a partisan preference for a reflexive political culture which never ceases to ask: 'What and where is power?' and, therefore, 'What and where is politics?'

But what it *doesn't* do is to justify a wholesale conflation of culture and politics. Conflicts over cultural autonomy and difference are not only political in the vague sense that culture *is* political when it becomes a site of contest and power play. These issues are also political in a narrower, perhaps even old-fashioned, sense. Material poverty; a lack of collective space (physical or mediated) which isn't commercially or politically administered; a welfare state which normalises lifestyles and biographies; the fiscal impoverishment of the unemployed; the temporal impoverishment of the employed: these are precisely the kinds of material factors that constrain the development of autonomous life forms and which demand a politics prepared to engage with legislative reform and questions of distributive justice. The general idea that cultural freedom is a political issue is hardly new in this sense.

But the most vexing question, of course, in the wake of postmodern debates (and the question most easily avoided by simply collapsing the distinction between culture and politics) is how demands for cultural autonomy can be politicised in the sense of being filtered upwards into the formal arenas of democratic will formation and policy formulation without violating those very principles of autonomy and difference in the process. One response would be cultural separatism – the fatalistic declaration of radical incommensurability. On the one hand, this does nothing to counter the inequitable distribution of the sorts of resources just mentioned and, in the anarchism of a cultural marketplace, encourages marginalisation and disenfranchisement. On the other hand, a conservative counterpart to this – in the guise of communitarianism – fares even worse insofar as it attempts to unify political communities under the auspices of a common good, a common cultural and ethical identity, which actually militates against reflexive critique and difference.

To assume that 'communities of fate' could ever be anything other than 'communities of difference' is utopian in the worst sense. What purely contextualist positions seem unable to deal with is that the scope of political issues and power relations in complex and interconnected societies outstrips, and becomes increasingly indifferent to, patterns of localised cultural narratives. Such narratives, in any case, are too fluid and dynamic ever to provide a stable foundation for political communities. At the same time, theorists including Giddens, Beck and Habermas all suspect (or hope) that the global scope of key problems in the risk society, most notably ecological issues, might provide at least some foundation for the establishment of a universal interest which could, under the sway of a cultural cosmopolitanism, nourish rather than erode tolerance and difference.[31] But we should tread with caution: the idea that ecological meltdown and other global risks could level or even lessen the stark antagonisms of strategic interests (something captured in Beck's simplistic and misguided soundbite: 'Poverty is hierarchic; smog is democratic')[32] rather than intensify them, *let alone* lend itself to a culturally universal notion of the common good, is idealistic at best and dangerous at worst.

For Habermas, attempting to deal with these questions entails framing the new sub-politics within a very old context – that of the liberal impulse to distinguish between rights and values coupled, of course, with the Marxian impulse towards exposing the tension between claim and reality. Perhaps this is the only way of envisaging a rejuvenated political culture that can exert power from *below* the threshold of a systematised formal democracy but *above* the incommensurable plurality of localised lifeworlds. The only universal Habermas permits critical theory to postulate outside the democratic deliberations of the public sphere itself – and a provisional one at that – is the most formal and minimal set of unavoidable presuppositions which, as speakers and hearers, we necessarily employ when we engage in discourse in 'good faith', believing in the possibility of unforced agreement, even if that agreement is ultimately confined to the principles by which we reach legitimate compromise. That the claims we raise could ideally be redeemed through dialogue; that we aim to make ourselves understood; and that we could somehow discriminate between genuine and coerced agreement: these provide, for Habermas, the necessary counterfactuals underpinning the messier realities of communication pursued in good faith. The universalism of the 'moral' point of view, for Habermas, remains strictly procedural in this sense: its work, which is always unfinished, is to try to make good those quaint liberal values of reciprocity and respect for the integrity and autonomy of the other. Modern liberalism went wrong, however, in imagining that autonomy derives from the essential rights of the unencumbered self. For Habermas, it derives instead from intersubjectivity itself.

As we have seen, Habermas argues that the fault-line of rights versus values must itself be the subject of democratic deliberation, given that the 'moral point of view' is always already ethically patterned within a political culture. So, for example, Habermas recognises that the welfare state does not simply *reflect* abstract rights but also contributes to their construction. These 'rights' therefore vary across welfare systems. Despite notable differences between, say, the Scandanavian and British models, most such systems embody cultural norms that privilege specific life forms, including the nuclear family, heterosexual marriage, long-term residence and a standardised working biography. For Habermas, though, this does not mean that the idea of welfare rights should be abandoned as some kind of patrician affront (which is the drift of many Leftist, anarchist and neo-conservative libertarian commentaries) but that we need to challenge the systemic fundamentalism that lends itself to such brittle normativity. The project of the welfare state needs to be continued, he says, at a 'higher level of reflection'.[33]

At the level of democratic culture itself, institutions of the political public sphere have tended to embody class-, race- and gender-specific cultures: the middle-class weighting of the new social and protest movements; the privileged demographic skew of the media and journalism professions; the lingering perceptions of patriarchy and xenophobia attaching to trade union movements; and the old-boy networks of the political parties. Again, these skews demand critical scrutiny rather than the easier option of dismissing them simply as out of touch and irrelevant. At the same time as Habermas's critical theory alerts us to the urgent project of reforming and rethinking these 'old' institutions, it also alerts us to the urgent project of rethinking politics itself by critically interrogating new sites of political deliberation and activity, that is, the proliferation of public spheres and tactical networks that, even as they refuse to play the language games of the old systemic elements of the state, the parties and the 'mass' media, operate in a context unavoidably shaped by them. Both 'projects' are always already 'unfinished'.

John Keane offers a pithy riposte to those who would argue that radical politics, in the guise of activist networks and subcultural movements, must operate outside the shadow of the 'state' and 'official' politics: civil society and the constitutional state, he argues, 'must become the condition of each other's democratisation'.[34] In all its circularity, that democratic ethic can only avoid pulling the rug from under its own feet if it starts from the ultimately pragmatic assertion that some things – such as the rights *and means* to assert difference, to define problems and to articulate perceptions of inequality – must be more equal than others. To that extent, universalism, one of the theoretical pillars of the 'old politics', cannot simply disappear from view in a globalising world, even if it has to be conceived in radically proceduralist and continuously reflexive terms. To assert this, of course, is to *assume* that progressive politics involves looking for ways of living with difference as opposed to eroding it or engaging the increasingly futile task of hiding from it.

But, of course, that may count as utopianism, one of the other theoretical pillars of the 'old' and perhaps defunct politics. It may be that the demise of providential reason, the rise of complex and manufactured risk, the realities of cultural difference and conflict, all militate against the re-emergence of utopian impulses behind political struggle. At the same time, as Beck and Giddens show in their discussions of the risk society, radical uncertainty renders all future-oriented thought counterfactual in any case, from apocalyptic sci-fi scenarios, through piecemeal risk assessment, right through to the utopian.

Interestingly, Habermas has made a recent intervention into the debates surrounding genetics[35] that unwittingly brings him into proximity with Beck and Giddens' concern for counterfactual thought and symbolic futures. It also brings his thinking into a connection with Thompson's emphasis on communication with the *absent* as the central problematic for democratic theory (Chapter 4), and even with recent post-structuralist discourses that frame human communication in terms of ghostly encounters.[36] Habermas engages in a philosophical speculation on the possible future scenario of 'liberal eugenics'. This is a scenario in which the genetic traits of the unborn child are subject not only to therapeutic interventions designed to avert serious disease or disability, but also to 'consumer' choice, such that parents may opt for particular talents or physical characteristics for their offspring. For Habermas, the real dangers of liberal eugenics are those of creating an irredeemably asymmetrical relationship between the generations. Except where the socialisation of a child has been so oppressive as to be classified as abusive, there is always scope for the adolescent to begin to reflect critically on its upbringing and to take ownership of the self and its biography. The idea that one can become the 'author' of one's own life is, at least, a powerful mythology or 'counterfactual ideal' that provides the backdrop for a 'normal' transition from childhood to adulthood and a subsequent sense of self-identity, autonomy and responsibility. According to Habermas, that mythology is imperilled by the prospect of parents, rather than simply serving as biological conduits for a more or less haphazard or incidental collection of traits, actually 'authoring' and selecting aspects of a child's genetic makeup. In contrast to socialisation processes, genetic influences cannot be appropriated and modified through critical reflection and so the danger is that individuals find it more difficult to take ownership of the self. Habermas fears for the ability of individuals to see themselves as responsible, in the last analysis, for their own actions, decisions and personalities. Such individuals may find it difficult not to imagine themselves to be 'authored' by someone else. So Habermas is not disturbed per se by technology's forays into new biological and reproductive territories: there is no natural boundary which medical technology is on the point of breaching. Rather, he is troubled by the prospect of seeing the horizontal relationship between generations – or, at least, the counterfactual ideal of an egalitarian relationship in which critical reflection, questioning and appropriation of life histories can occur – being displaced by a new set of inter-generational relations for which there is no precedent. And those inter-generational relations are critically important for both individual and collective groups and their sense of place in the world. Individuals can selectively appropriate or reject aspects of their heritage and socialisation within modern societies. So too, entire generations can simultaneously learn from *and* criticise or try to rectify the actions of previous generations. According to Habermas, however, the scenario of liberal eugenics raises serious questions about the structures of autonomy and responsibility within future generations.

But we should also acknowledge that once the technology has presented us with such a fork in the road, the current generation will have to be responsible for *whichever* path it takes. The decision to *disallow* embryo selection or genetic intervention for non-therapeutic reasons – to improve longevity or to enhance particular attributes, say – and to refrain from funding research and development in this field, is in principle one that future generations may look back on critically. In reflexive modernity, we face the problem of 'playing God' whichever way we look. But whilst Habermas seems to miss this rather basic point, his own emphasis on discourse ethics can, I think, be useful here. The only way out of the dilemma is to engage in critical dialogue with future generations. Of course, that's not a literal possibility. But in current debates in genetics, future generations are already routinely invoked: they already have their spokespeople. Now, we could be content to conceive these debates as counterfactual thought experiments, after Giddens and Beck. We could, following Thompson, acknowledge that our communications with future generations are 'quasi-interactions' funnelled through expert systems of mediation where, for example, 'public scientists' like Lord Robert Winston front television shows which explain the issues at stake, or movies like *Gattaca* spark off debates between friends: these mediated representations are, of course, the sine qua non of a contemporary public sphere that makes onerous demands on citizens who are expected to form opinions on an array of immensely complex topics. We could instead adopt the ironic stance which is de rigueur in post-structuralist discourse and proclaim that our communications with the not-yet-born, like those with the dead, are in any case no more problematic than those we convene amongst the living: in this case, any concerns we may have about the quality of the information or the balance of viewpoints in these media representations would be a rather meaningless gesture based on a fantasy of 'authentic communication'. Or we could try to imagine the relevance of discourse ethics to these impossible encounters. Given that we do not know them and that, like us, they will probably speak with many voices, aren't 'future generations' best, if always imperfectly, served by the most diverse range possible of representatives, representations and discursive frameworks? Aren't they best served by the existence of spaces of debate that are independent of special market or political interests? We absolutely *require* a diverse communication mix (web-logs, lobby-group communications, public-service documentaries, movies, poetry, radical media publications, stand-up comedy and so forth) noisily kicking the topic around before we can even begin to call it a 'public sphere'. This plurality of communicative forms (different genres, different motivations, different goals) does not, in itself, guarantee the transition from 'noise' to 'dialogue'. But without such diversity of form and perspective, it is impossible to claim sincerely that we are proceeding with the interests of future generations in mind. If Giddens and Beck teach us the importance of counterfactual thinking, Habermas reminds us that counterfactual thinking is something that must occur 'out loud' amid the crossfire of diverse perspectives. Against those readings of Habermas which emphasise his ('misguided') attachment to the principles of co-presence (as if 'real' communication required participants to share a common spatial or temporal location), it is possible to see how discourse ethics and 'counterfactual thinking' can, in fact, be complementary impulses.

But what about utopian counterfactualism? It may be the case that apocalyptic images of ecological destruction, pervasive hi-tech warfare and acute global poverty are more persuasive given that those developments are already in full swing. The question of how to draw utopian energies from all this 'may be objectively obscure', says Habermas. 'Obscurity is nonetheless also a function of a society's assessment of its own readiness to take action. What is at stake is Western culture's confidence in itself.'[37] What's at stake, perhaps, is not simply Western culture's confidence in itself, in the idealistic sense that implies. Rather, what may be at stake is the ability to imagine, build and renew institutions, both formal and informal, which can draw from the shreds of cultural fragmentation some alliances and affiliations capable of challenging systemic as well as lifeworld fundamentalism, and countering the fatalism which those apocalyptic and persuasive images of destruction, coercion and conflict seem to engender.

Habermas is so often associated with a touching, naïve and one-dimensional faith in the healing powers of communicative rationality, as if the world could be set to rights if only the public sphere could be made over in the image of the philosophy seminar, and if only unruly citizens could be helped to see through the 'performative contradictions' of their less than rational, agonistic utterances. As this discussion has hopefully shown, I think we can and should discern a radically different legacy from the Habermasian discourse of the public sphere. It teaches us, in fact, that critical theory must be self-limiting yet reconstructive: rather than setting the world to rights above the everyday struggles and conflicts of citizens themselves, it should set its sights on casting those struggles and conflicts in new light, suggesting where our aspirations for common ground and resolution might take us and, indeed, where we should avoid them taking us. If the Habermasian discourse of public sphere teaches us anything, it is just how daunting are the tasks that befall the democratic imagination, and just how precarious are its hopes.

Notes

1 EXCAVATIONS: THE HISTORY OF A CONCEPT

1. J. Habermas, *The Structural Transformation of the Public Sphere: An Inquiry into a Category of Bourgeois Society*, trans. T. Burger (Cambridge: Polity, 1989 [1962]), p. 7.
2. Ibid., pp. 15–17.
3. Although Habermas writes as a social theorist rather than historian, the 'grand narrative' of political centralisation is in fact treated with more precision and with more acknowledgement of uneven developments than I can do justice to here.
4. Habermas, *Structural Transformation*, p. 11.
5. Ibid., p. 18.
6. Ibid., p. 24.
7. Ibid., p. 15. Given the explosive consequences Habermas attributes to the advent of mass printing, it is curious that communications media have remained so glaringly under-theorised in his work overall. I address this blind spot in Chapter 4.
8. Habermas, *Structural Transformation*, pp. 16–20.
9. Ibid., p. 24.
10. B. Anderson, *Imagined Communities: Reflections on the Origin and Spread of Nationalism* (London: Verso, 1991).
11. Habermas, *Structural Transformation*, p. 21.
12. Habermas does not discuss the thesis, often dismissed as 'technological determinism', that there was actually something inherent in the nature of this new medium that contributed to the demise of representative publicness. See M. McLuhan, *Understanding Media: The Extensions of Man* (London: Routledge, 1994 [1964]).
13. Habermas, *Structural Transformation*, p. 24.
14. Ibid., p. 25.
15. Ibid., p. 34.
16. Ibid., pp. 37–8.
17. Ibid., p. 33.
18. Ibid., pp. 49–50.
19. Ibid., pp. 3, 52.
20. Ibid., p. 27.
21. Ibid., pp. 32, 39–41.
22. Ibid., p. 54.
23. Ibid., p. 42.
24. Ibid., p. 37.
25. Ibid., pp. 52–5.
26. Ibid., p. 28.
27. Ibid., pp. 73–9.
28. Ibid., p. 53.

29. In Britain, 'Licensing Acts' during the sixteenth and seventeenth centuries heavily restricted the development of publishing enterprises and served as a means of censorship; a system of stamp taxes imposed upon the press during the eighteenth century and the first half of the nineteenth century simultaneously restricted legitimate circulation and encouraged an oppositional underground press; libel and sedition laws further inflamed controversies over press freedom.
30. Habermas, *Structural Transformation*, pp. 60–1.
31. Ibid., p. 64.
32. Ibid., pp. 58–9.
33. Ibid., p. 65.
34. Ibid., pp. 66–7.
35. Ibid., pp. 67–71.
36. Ibid., p. 73.
37. Ibid., p. 89.
38. Ibid., pp. 90–1.
39. Ibid., pp. 91–2.
40. Ibid., pp. 93–4.
41. Ibid., p. 94.
42. Ibid., p. 99.
43. Ibid., p. 103.
44. Ibid., pp. 104–6.
45. Ibid., p. 106.
46. Ibid., pp. 109–10.
47. Ibid., p. 111.
48. See J. Habermas, *The Inclusion of the Other: Studies in Political Theory*, trans. C. Cronin and P. de Greiff (Cambridge, Mass.: MIT Press, 1998).
49. Habermas, *Structural Transformation*, p. 119.
50. Ibid., p. 121.
51. Ibid., pp. 117–22.
52. Ibid., pp. 122–3.
53. K. Marx, 'A Contribution to the Critique of Hegel's Philosophy of Right: Introduction' [1843–4] in *Early Writings*, trans. R. Livingstone and G. Benton (Harmondsworth: Penguin Books, 1992), pp. 253–4.
54. Habermas, *Structural Transformation*, pp. 128–9.
55. Ibid., pp. 131–2.
56. Ibid., p. 131.
57. Ibid., p. 133.
58. Ibid., pp. 133–3.
59. Ibid., p. 136.
60. Ibid., p. 140.
61. Ibid., p. 142.
62. Ibid., p. 144.
63. Ibid., p. 146.
64. Ibid., p. 151.
65. Ibid., p. 152.
66. Ibid., pp. 154–5.
67. Ibid., p. 155.
68. Ibid., p. 157.

69. J. Habermas, *Legitimation Crisis* (London: Heinemann 1976).

70. Habermas, *Structural Transformation*, p. 156.

71. Ibid., p. 157.

72. Ibid., p. 159.

73. Ibid., p. 159.

74. Ibid., p. 160.

75. T.W. Adorno, 'Free time', in *The Culture Industry: Selected Essays on Mass Culture*, ed. J.M. Bernstein (London: Routledge, 1991).

76. In view of the common criticism that Habermas overplays the ideologically integrative effects of the culture industry, it is worth noting the attention he devotes to these material questions. His citation of H.P. Bahrdt reinforces this: 'The reciprocity of the public and private spheres is disturbed ... not ... because the city dweller is mass man per se and hence no longer has any sensibility for the cultivation of the private sphere; but because he no longer succeeds in getting an overview of the ever more complicated life of the city as a whole in such fashion that it is really public for him. The more the city as a whole is transformed into a barely penetrable jungle, the more he withdraws into his sphere of privacy which in turn is extended ever further.' *Structural Transformation*, p. 159.

77. Habermas, *Structural Transformation*, pp. 157–9.

78. Ibid., p. 166.

79. Ibid., p. 175.

80. Ibid., p. 171.

81. Ibid., p. 164.

82. Ibid., pp. 163, 170–1.

83. 'In comparison with printed communications the programmes sent by the new media curtail the reactions of their recipients in a peculiar way. They draw the eyes and ears of the public under their spell but at the same time, by taking away its distance, place it under "tutelage", which is to say they deprive it of the opportunity to say something and to disagree.' Ibid., p. 171.

84. J. Habermas, 'Further reflections on the public sphere', in C. Calhoun (ed.), *Habermas and the Public Sphere* (Cambridge, Mass.: MIT Press, 1992), p. 439.

85. For example, in a recent discussion of Kant he makes the following remark: 'He [Kant] could not forsee the structural transformation of the bourgeois public sphere into a semantically degenerated public sphere dominated by the electronic mass media and pervaded by images and virtual realities. He could scarcely imagine that this milieu of 'conversational' enlightenment could be adapted both to nonverbal indoctrination and to deception *by means of* language.' Habermas, *Inclusion of the Other*, p. 176.

86. Habermas, *Structural Transformation*, p. 189. Today the situation is more complex. Advances in digital technology have made smaller-scale and niche broadcasting ('narrowcasting') more viable. But the implications for diversity are not all positive as demographics and communities of low priority to advertsisers tend to get marginalised. Moreover, even today, television remains a 'mass medium' in many respects. In my

current home country, Aotearoa/New Zealand, for example, a small, widely dispersed population means that even mainstream broadcasting is a less than lucrative business.

87. Ibid., pp. 165–6.
88. Ibid., p. 166.
89. Ibid., p. 182.
90. Ibid., pp. 166–7.
91. Ibid., p. 177.
92. Ibid., p. 176. Tripartite corporatism ('beer and sandwiches at 10 Downing Street' was the quaint British metonym) bringing unions, corporations and government into negotiation has, of course, been replaced by the domineering presence of the professional lobbyists, and the shadowy networks of corporate hospitality in most Western democracies.
93. C. Offe, *Contradictions of the Welfare State* (London: Hutchinson, 1984).
94. Habermas, *Structural Transformation*, pp. 203–5.
95. Ibid., p. 211.
96. Ibid., p. 202.
97. Ibid., p. 213
98. Ibid., p. 201.
99. Ibid., p. 237.
100. Ibid., p. 241.
101. Ibid., pp. 226–7.
102. Ibid., p. 210.
103. Ibid., p. 209.
104. Ibid., p. 227.
105. Ibid., p. 208.

2   DISCURSIVE TESTING: THE PUBLIC SPHERE AND ITS CRITICS

1. J. Habermas, 'Further reflections on the public sphere', in C. Calhoun (ed.), *Habermas and the Public Sphere* (Cambridge, Mass.: MIT Press, 1992), p. 438.
2. C. Calhoun, 'Introduction', in Calhoun (ed.), *Habermas and the Public Sphere*, p. 33.
3. G. Eley, 'Nations, publics and political cultures: placing Habermas in the nineteenth century', in Calhoun (ed.), *Habermas and the Public Sphere*, p. 307.
4. K. Baker, 'Defining the public sphere in eighteenth century France: variations on a theme by Habermas', in Calhoun (ed.), *Habermas and the Public Sphere*, pp. 191–2.
5. As Eley puts it: 'It's open to question how far these [alternative public spheres] were simply derivative of the liberal model ... and how far they possessed their own dynamics of emergence and peculiar forms of internal life.' Eley, 'Nations, publics and political cultures', p. 304.
6. By which I mean that their principles, objectives and *modus operandi* did not, according to revisionist historiography, diverge so greatly from those of the bourgeois public sphere that their exclusion from the

narrative could be justified on the grounds that they were unrecognisable *as* 'public spheres' in the sense intended by Habermas; nor, on the other hand, did their principles, objectives and *modus operandi* simply conform to those of the bourgeois public sphere sufficiently to justify absorbing them into the bourgeois model rather than according them a distinctive place in the narrative.

7. E.P. Thompson's *The Making of the English Working Class* (Harmondsworth: Penguin, 1968) provides a different and complementary historical emphasis in this sense.

8. Nancy Fraser, 'Rethinking the public sphere: a contribution to the critique of actually existing democracy', in Calhoun (ed.), *Habermas and the Public Sphere*, p. 116.

9. Women's suffrage began in New Zealand with women being granted the vote in 1893. Very few other countries (Australia and Scandinavia) followed suit before the First World War.

10. Fraser, 'Rethinking the public sphere', p. 113.

11. Habermas is frequently accused of fudging the distinction between theory and practice in *Structural Transformation*. See, for example, R. Holub, *Habermas: Critic in the Public Sphere* (London: Routledge, 1991), pp. 7–8. But I think a careful study of the text reveals quite clearly that it is a story of unfulfilled promise.

12. M. Ryan, 'Gender and public access: women's politics in nineteenth-century America', in Calhoun (ed.), *Habermas and the Public Sphere*, pp. 262–3.

13. D. Zaret, 'Religion, science, and printing in the public spheres in seventeenth-century England', in Calhoun (ed.), *Habermas and the Public Sphere*, p. 215.

14. In response to Zaret's critique, Habermas says the following: 'I think I have in the meantime … changed my own framework so that the permanent autonomy of cultural developments is taken more accurately into account. Simply, I have incorporated a bit more of Max Weber and of changes in religious thought, moral belief systems, the impact of the authority of science in secularized, everyday practices, even as pacesetters of social change. So I'm more open today to integrating some of the evidence of more recent anthropological approaches in history.' 'Concluding remarks', in Calhoun (ed.), *Habermas and the Public Sphere*, p. 464.

15. P. Hohendahl, 'Critical theory, public sphere and culture: Jürgen Habermas and his critics', *New German Critique*, vol. 16 (1979).

16. Ibid., p. 104.

17. O. Negt and A. Kluge, 'The public sphere and experience: selections', trans. P. Labanyi, *October*, no. 46 (Fall, 1988 [1972]).

18. P. Hohendahl, 'Critical theory, public sphere and culture', pp. 105–6.

19. Ibid., p. 105.

20. Negt and Kluge, 'The public sphere and experience', p. 61.

21. Ibid., p. 63.

22. Ibid., p. 65.

23. See Holub, *Habermas: Critic in the Public Sphere*, pp. 78–105.

24. N. Garnham, 'The media and the public sphere', in Calhoun (ed.), *Habermas and the Public Sphere*, pp. 361–2.
25. Ibid., pp. 362–4.
26. Ibid., pp. 364–5.
27. Fraser, 'Rethinking the public sphere', p. 109.
28. Ibid., p. 111.
29. Ibid., p. 117.
30. Ibid., pp. 119 (emphases added).
31. Ibid., p. 120.
32. Ibid., p. 121.
33. Ibid., p. 117.
34. Ibid., p. 122.
35. Ibid., p. 123.
36. Ibid., p. 124.
37. T. Gitlin, 'Public sphere or public sphericules?', in T. Liebes and J. Curran (eds), *Media, Ritual, Identity* (London: Routledge, 1998), pp. 168–75.
38. Fraser, 'Rethinking the public sphere', p. 118.
39. Ibid., pp. 128–9.
40. See S. Benhabib, *Situating the Self: Gender, Community and Postmodernism in Contemporary Ethics*, (Cambridge: Polity Press, 1992).
41. Fraser, 'Rethinking the public sphere', pp. 129–30.
42. Ibid., p. 130.
43. Ibid., p. 131.
44. R. Pfeufer Kahn, 'The problem of power in Habermas', *Human Studies*, vol. 11, no. 4 (1988), pp. 375–6.
45. B. Latour, 'Whose cosmos, which cosmopolitics? Comments on the peace terms of Ulrich Beck', <http://www.ensmp.fr/~latour/articles/article/92-BECK-CK.html> (2004).
46. I do not intend to overstate the match between Latour and Habermas's perspectives. Latour actually mounts a more radical critique of liberal humanism than Habermas (one that merits serious attention) and asks us to put aside the illusion (at best) or instruction (at worst) that non-human interests be eliminated from the public sphere. To acknowledge that the Enlightenment view of humans as emancipated from their 'gods' is unrealistic and ethnocentric is one thing. It is quite another to elucidate the conditions under which communication *between human beings* across these cultural and religious zones might actually ensue. That is where Habermas's contribution is stronger than Latour's.
47. J.D. Peters, 'Distrust of representation: Habermas on the public sphere', *Media, Culture and Society*, vol. 15 (1993).
48. Ibid., p. 562.
49. Ibid., p. 563.
50. Ibid., p. 564.
51. Ibid., p. 566.
52. Ibid., p. 546.
53. R. Sennett, *The Fall of Public Man* (London: Faber and Faber, 1986 [1977]), p. 270.
54. Ibid., p. 276.
55. Peters, 'Distrust of representation', p. 565.

56. B. Anderson, *Imagined Communities: Reflections on the Origin and Spread of Nationalism* (London: Verso, 1991).
57. Peters, 'Distrust of representation', p. 565.
58. Ibid., p. 567.
59. M. Warner, 'The mass public and the mass subject', in B. Robbins (ed.), *The Phantom Public Sphere* (Minneapolis: University of Minnesota Press, 1993), p. 239.
60. Ibid., p. 242.
61. Ibid., p. 241.
62. Ibid., p. 247.
63. Ibid., p. 247–8.
64. Ibid., p. 241.
65. Ibid., p. 253.
66. Ibid., p. 255.
67. Habermas, 'Concluding remarks', p. 466.
68. U. Eco, *The Role of the Reader: Explorations in the Semiotics of Texts* (Bloomington: Indiana University Press, 1984).

3   RECONFIGURATIONS:
THE PUBLIC SPHERE SINCE *STRUCTURAL TRANSFORMATION*

1. J. Habermas, *Toward a Rational Society: Student Protest, Science and Politics*, trans. J. Shapiro (Cambridge: Polity Press, 1987 [1962]).
2. J. Habermas, 'The scientisation of politics and public opinion', in *Toward a Rational Society*, p. 68.
3. J. Habermas, 'The university in a democracy', in *Toward a Rational Society*, p. 6.
4. Habermas, 'The scientisation of politics and public opinion', pp. 62–3.
5. See also T. McCarthy, *The Critical Theory of Jürgen Habermas* (Cambridge: Polity Press), p. 11.
6. Habermas, 'The scientisation of politics and public opinion', pp. 68ff.
7. The popular use of the term 'pragmatism' in contemporary political culture should not be confused with the 'pragmatistic' model of politics discussed by Habermas in *Toward a Rational Society*. This 'pragmatism' rejects the technocratic model and overlaps with Habermas's own ideals of a political culture based on the interaction between experts and a critically debating public concerned with norms as well as facts. Habermas criticises the pragmatistic model, however, because, as he puts it, it 'neglects the specific logical characteristics and the social preconditions for the reliable translation of scientific information into the ordinary language of practice and inversely for a translation from the context of practical questions back into the specialised language of technical and strategic recommendations '. 'The scientisation of politics and public opinion', p. 70.
8. T. W. Adorno et al., *The Positivist Dispute in German Sociology* (London: Heinemann, 1977 [1969]).
9. Habermas, 'The university in a democracy', pp. 6–7.

10. J. Habermas, 'Technical progress and the social life-world', in *Toward a Rational Society*, pp. 57–8.
11. Habermas, 'The university in a democracy', p. 7.
12. Holub, *Habermas: Critic in the Public Sphere*, pp. 78–105. See also J. Habermas, *Philosophical and Political Profiles*, trans. F. Lawrence (London: Heinemann, 1983), pp. 165–70.
13. Holub, *Habermas: Critic in the Public Sphere*, p. 85.
14. J. Habermas, 'Technology and science as "ideology"', in *Toward a Rational Society*.
15. Habermas, 'The scientisation of politics and public opinion', p. 73.
16. J. Habermas, *The Theory of Communicative Action vol. 1: Reason and the Rationalisation of Society*, trans. T. McCarthy (Cambridge: Polity Press, 1991 [1981]), pp. 90–3.
17. J. Habermas, *Moral Consciousness and Communicative Action*, trans. C. Lenhardt and S. Weber Nicholsen (Cambridge: Polity Press, 1990 [1983]), p. 9.
18. J. Habermas, *The Philosophical Discourse of Modernity*, trans. F. Lawrence (Cambridge: Polity Press, 1987).
19. J. Habermas, *Communication and the Evolution of Society*, trans. T. McCarthy (Cambridge: Polity Press, 1984 [1976]), pp. 1–68.
20. Habermas, *Communication and the Evolution of Society*, p. 68.
21. Ibid., pp. 50–1.
22. Habermas, *The Theory of Communicative Action vol. 1*, p. 297.
23. Habermas, *Communication and the Evolution of Society*, p. 64.
24. Habermas, *The Theory of Communicative Action vol. 1*, p. 303.
25. Ibid., p. 302.
26. Unlike 'strategic action' which 'remains indifferent with respect to its motivational conditions.' Habermas, *Communication and the Evolution of Society*, p. 118.
27. M. Jay, 'Habermas and Modernism', in R. Bernstein (ed.), *Habermas and Modernity* (Cambridge: Polity Press, 1985).
28. Habermas, *Communication and the Evolution of Society*, p. 65.
29. See R. Blaug, *Democracy, Real and Ideal: Discourse Ethics and Radical Politics* (Albany. State University of New York Press, 1999). Blaug has rightly argued that the metaphor of a critical 'yardstick' often claimed for Habermas's ideal speech situation is misleading. There are too many variables to be able to measure or compare various actual speech situations with the kind of precision this objectivist metaphor implies. However, I'm not convinced by his suggestion that this renders the notion entirely meaningless. The 'ideal speech situation' should not be conceived as a calibration tool for the social scientist, but rather, as a framework for understanding the processes by which actual participants work at the challenge of *better* communication.
30. See J.D. Peters, *Speaking into the Air: A History of the Idea of Communication* (Chicago: University of Chicago Press, 1999). Peters mounts an elegant, but unnecessarily extreme, critique of reciprocity.
31. 'Our first sentence expresses unequivocally the intention of universal and unconstrained consensus.' J. Habermas, *Knowledge and Human Interests*, trans. J. Shapiro (Cambridge: Polity Press, 1987 [1968], p. 314.

32. Habermas, *The Theory of Communicative Action vol. 1*, p. 95.
33. J. Habermas, *The Theory of Communicative Action vol. 2: Lifeworld and System: The Critique of Functionalist Reason*, trans. T. McCarthy (Cambridge: Polity Press, 1987[1981]), p. 119.
34. Ibid., p. 125.
35. Ibid., p. 124.
36. Ibid., p. 138.
37. Ibid., pp. 262–3. I acknowledge that I am glossing over Habermas's deeply controversial adoption of the vocabulary of systems theory. A forgiving reading of the system–lifeworld model is one that sees them not as discrete spheres of society but as signifiers of the relative prevalence of the various 'media' – money, strategic power and communicative action – in social interactions. See L. Ray, *Rethinking Critical Theory: Emancipation in the Age of Social Movements* (London: Sage, 1993).
38. Habermas, *The Theory of Communicative Action vol. 2*, p. 148.
39. Ibid., p. 180.
40. Ibid., p. 184.
41. Ibid., p. 178.
42. Ibid., pp. 301–2.
43. Ibid., p. 302.
44. Ibid., p. 392.
45. Ibid., p. 394.
46. Ibid., p. 398.
47. Habermas, *The Philosophical Discourse of Modernity*; see also J. Habermas, *Postmetaphysical Thinking: Philosophical Essays*, trans. W.M. Hohengarten (Cambridge, Mass.: MIT Press, 1992).
48. Habermas, *Knowledge and Human Interests*.
49. J. Habermas, *The Inclusion of the Other: Studies in Political Theory*, trans. C. Cronin and P. de Greiff (Cambridge, Mass.: MIT Press, 1998), p. 4.
50. Ibid., pp. 43–4.
51. J. Habermas, *The Future of Human Nature* (Cambridge: Polity Press, 2003), p. 39.
52. Habermas, *The Inclusion of the Other*, p. 43.
53. Ibid., p. 41 (emphases added).
54. Habermas, *The Future of Human Nature*, p. 4.
55. Ibid., p. 73.
56. J. Habermas, *Between Facts and Norms: Contributions to a Discourse Theory of Law and Democracy*, trans. W. Rehg (Cambridge: Polity Press, 1996).
57. J. Habermas, 'Postscript to *Between Facts and Norms*', in M. Deflem (ed.), *Habermas, Modernity and Law* (London: Sage, 1996), p. 139.
58. Habermas, *The Inclusion of the Other*, p. 257.
59. Habermas, 'Postscript to *Between Facts and Norms*', p. 138.
60. That's not to say that citizens can be obliged to exercise their public autonomy communicatively rather than strategically. The point Habermas is making, however, is that citizens can only hope to bridge the gap between morality and law (and go beyond the role of mere legal *subjects*) if they are open to mutual accommodation in legal norms that operate at greater and greater levels of abstraction in order to bridge

competing interests: 'To this extent, constitutional democracy depends on the motivations of a population *accustomed* to liberty, motivations that cannot be generated by administrative measures.' Ibid., p. 147.

61. Habermas, *The Inclusion of the Other*, p. 257.
62. Habermas, 'Postscript to *Between Facts and Norms*', p. 142.
63. Habermas, *The Inclusion of the Other*, p. 101.
64. Habermas, 'Postscript to *Between Facts and Norms*', p. 141.
65. Peters, *Speaking into the Air*.
66. E. Laclau and C. Mouffe, *Hegemony and Socialist Strategy: Towards a Radical Democratic Politics* (London: Verso, 1985).
67. E. Laclau, *Emancipation(s)* (London: Verso, 1996), p. xiii.
68. Habermas, *The Inclusion of the Other*, pp. 109ff.
69. Ibid., pp. 112–13.
70. Ibid., p. 117.
71. There is not space here to discuss Habermas's writings on immigration. See especially *The Inclusion of the Other*, pp. 228–35. He mounts a scathing critique of First World governments, especially in Europe (with special contempt reserved for his home nation), for their treatment of refugees, for the air of benevolence that occludes questions of responsibility in the historical context of colonialism, for their dogmatic but hypocritical refusal to accept the legitimacy of economic refugees and their xenophobic obsession with cultural assimilation beyond what could legitimately be demanded as a 'functional' necessity.
72. C. Cronin and P. de Greiff, 'Translators' Introduction', in Habermas, *The Inclusion of the Other*, p. xxviii.
73. Habermas, *The Inclusion of the Other*, pp. 221–2.
74. Ibid., p. 40.
75. Ibid., p. 221. This sense of conditional respect can be a troublesome dynamic in the case of indigenous peoples, such as the *tangata whenua* or 'people of the land' in New Zealand, whose cultural practices tend to be treated with sincere respect by the majority culture insofar as they fit the dominant frame – compatible with eco-tourism – of traditionalism, rurality and spiritualism, but whose underlying diversity, flux, and complex connections with global cultures and subcultures prove difficult to frame.
76. M. Castells, *The Rise of the Network Society*, 2nd edn. (Oxford: Blackwell, 2000).
77. A. Appadurai, *Modernity at Large: Cultural Dimensions of Globalization* (Minneapolis: University of Minnesota Press, 1996).
78. M. Wark, *Virtual Geography: Living with Global Media Events* (Bloomington: Indiana University Press, 1994).
79. Habermas, *The Inclusion of the Other*, p. 145.
80. C. Gilligan, *In a Different Voice: Psychological Theory and Women's Development* (Cambridge, Mass.: Harvard University Press, 1982).
81. D. Haraway, *Simians, Cyborgs and Women: The Reinvention of Nature* (New York: Routledge, 1991), pp. 149–81.
82. G. Deleuze and F. Guattari, *A Thousand Plateaus: Capitalism and Schizophrenia* (Minneapolis: University of Minnesota Press, 1987).

4   MEDIATIONS:
FROM THE COFFEE HOUSE TO THE INTERNET CAFÉ

1. J. Habermas, *The Theory of Communicative Action vol. 2: Lifeworld and System: The Critique of Functionalist Reason*, trans. T. McCarthy (Cambridge: Polity Press, 1987 [1981]), p. 390.
2. J.D. Peters, *Speaking into the Air: A History of the Idea of Communication* (Chicago: University of Chicago Press, 1999).
3. J.B. Thompson, *Ideology and Modern Culture: Critical Theory in the Era of Mass Communication* (Cambridge: Polity Press, 1990); 'The theory of the public sphere', *Theory, Culture and Society*, vol. 10, no. 3 (1993); 'Social theory and the media', in D. Crowley and D. Mitchell (eds), *Communication Theory Today* (Cambridge: Polity Press, 1994); *The Media and Modernity: A Social Theory of the Media* (Cambridge: Polity Press, 1995).
4. See, for example, M. Poster, *The Second Media Age* (Cambridge: Polity Press, 1995).
5. Thompson, *Ideology and Modern Culture*, p. 120.
6. Ibid., p. 120.
7. Ibid., pp. 228ff.
8. Thompson, 'Social theory and the media', p. 35.
9. Ibid., p. 36.
10. Ibid., p. 37; see also P. Scannell, 'Public service broadcasting: the history of a concept', in A. Goodwin and G. Whannel (eds), *Understanding Television* (London: Routledge, 1992), pp. 11–29.
11. Thompson, *Ideology and Modern Culture*, p. 225.
12. F. Jameson, *Postmodernism, or the Cultural Logic of Late Capitalism* (London: Verso, 1990).
13. A. Giddens, *Modernity and Self-Identity: Self and Society in the Late Modern Age* (Cambridge: Polity Press, 1991), pp. 187–8.
14. It is important that we do not make the ontological assumption that physical distance is always a problem for which communication technologies such as the phone offer a *remedy*. The telephone may help to overcome the physical distance of two people; but the phone can also be used to *create* distance between the user and the people in his immediate physical vicinity; and it can be used to *exploit* distance, as in the case of the text-message flirting between two people only yards apart. Distance is not always a pathology, and communication technologies are not always used to overcome it.
15. Giddens, *Modernity and Self-Identity*, p. 33.
16. I shall return to this issue in the final chapter.
17. Thompson, 'The theory of the public sphere', pp. 186–7.
18. See, for example, P. Scannell, 'Public service broadcasting and modern public life', in P. Scannell et al. (eds), *Culture and Power* (London: Sage, 1991); J. Keane, *The Media and Democracy* (Cambridge: Polity Press, 1991); P. Golding and G. Murdock, 'Culture, communications and political economy', in J. Curran and M. Gurevitch (eds), *Mass Media and Society*, 2nd edn (London: Arnold, 1991); P. Dahlgren and C. Sparks

(eds), *Communication and Citizenship: Journalism and the Public Sphere* (London: Sage, 1991).

19. N. Negroponte, *Being Digital* (London: Coronet, 1996); H. Schiller, 'The global information highway: project for an ungovernable world', in J. Brook and I. Boal (eds), *Resisting the Virtual Life: The Culture and Politics of Information* (San Francisco: City Light Books, 1995).

20. Thompson, *Ideology and Modern Culture*, p. 115; Thompson, 'Social theory and the media', pp. 39–40.

21. J. Habermas, *The Structural Transformation of the Public Sphere: An Inquiry into a Category of Bourgeois Society*, trans. T. Burger (Cambridge: Polity Press, 1989 [1962]), p. 195.

22. Thompson, *Ideology and Modern Culture*, pp. 231–2.

23. Ibid., pp. 245–6. A neat counterexample would be the development of sophisticated databases which enable corporations and now political parties to deploy 'direct mailing' techniques. Dividing households into marketing categories enables parties to produce tailor-made literature and reduce the risks involved in the *diffuse* circulation of media symbols.

24. Thompson, 'Social theory and the media', p. 40.

25. Ibid., p. 41.

26. D. Kellner, *Media Culture: Cultural Studies, Identity and Politics Between the Modern and the Postmodern* (London: Routledge, 1995), pp. 198–228.

27. E. Said, *Culture and Imperialism* (London: Vintage, 1994).

28. Thompson, 'Social theory and the media', p. 41.

29. P. Schlesinger, 'Europe's contradictory communicative space', *Dædalus*, vol. 123, no. 2 (1994), pp. 34–5.

30. N. Garnham, 'The media and the public sphere', in C. Calhoun (ed.), *Habermas and the Public Sphere* (Cambridge, Mass.: MIT Press, 1992), p. 371.

31. D. Held, 'Democracy and the new international order', in D. Archibugi and D. Held (eds), *Cosmopolitan Democracy: An Agenda for a New World Order* (Cambridge: Polity Press, 1995), p. 112.

32. Thompson, 'Social theory and the media', p. 31.

33. J. Habermas, 'What does socialism mean today? The rectifying revolution and the need for new thinking on the Left', *New Left Review*, no. 183 (1990), pp. 19–20 (emphases added).

34. C. Calhoun, 'Populist politics, communications media and large scale societal integration', *Sociological Theory*, vol. 6 (Fall, 1988), p. 244.

35. For a useful survey of this literature, see N. Stevenson, *Understanding Media Cultures: Social Theory and Mass Communication* (London: Sage 1995), pp. 75–113.

36. J. Habermas, *The Future of Human Nature* (Cambridge: Polity Press, 2003), p. 121.

37. Consider, for example, the thoroughly Habermasian virtues of internal scepticism and 'reflexive publicity' (Chapter 1) expressed in the following from a *Wired* editorial: 'Are we living in the middle of a great revolution, or are we just members of another arrogant élite talking to ourselves? Are we a powerful new kind of community or just a mass of people hooked up to machines? Do we share goals and ideals, or are we

just another hot market ready for exploitation by America's ravenous corporations? ... Can we build a new kind of politics? Can we construct a more civil society with our powerful technologies? Are we extending the evolution of freedom among human beings? Or are we nothing more than a great, wired babble, pissing into the digital wind?' J. Katz, 'Birth of a digital nation', *Wired*, vol. 5.04 (1996).

38. A European Commission policy document proclaiming that 'new services and technologies empower the consumer *and* the citizen', but which never explains what the distinction is, is a typical example of such a comfortable rhetorical elision. European Commission, *Convergence Green Paper: Working Document*, <http://www.ispo.cec.be/convergencegp/gpworkdoc.html> (1998).

39. H. Rheingold, *Virtual Community: Finding Connection in a Computerized World* (London: Vintage, 1993).

40. B. Connery, 'IMHO: authority and egalitarian rhetoric in the virtual coffeehouse', in D. Porter (ed.), *Internet Culture* (London: Routledge, 1997).

41. D. Kellner, 'Techno-politics, new technologies, and the new public spheres', <http://www.uta.edu/huma/illuminations> (1998).

42. M. Poster, *The Second Media Age* (Cambridge: Polity Press, 1995); *What's the Matter with the Internet?* (Minneapolis: University of Minnesota Press, 2001).

43. M. Poster, 'Cyberdemocracy: internet and the public sphere', in Porter (ed.), *Internet Culture*, p. 214.

44. L. Manovich, *The Language of New Media* (Cambridge, Mass.: MIT Press, 2001).

45. D. Schiller, *Digital Capitalism: Networking the Global Market System* (Cambridge, Mass.: MIT Press, 1999).

46. J. Baudrillard, *In the Shadow of the Silent Majorities, or, the End of the Social and Other Essays*, trans. P. Foss (New York: Semiotexte, 1983); D. Morley and K. Robins, *Spaces of Identity: Global Media, Electronic Landscapes and Cultural Boundaries* (London: Routledge, 1995), pp. 194–5.

47. P. Lunenfeld, *Snap to Grid: A User's Guide to Digital Arts, Media and Cultures* (Cambridge, Mass.: MIT Press, 2000).

48. G.P. Landow, *Hypertext 2.0* (Baltimore: Johns Hopkins University Press, 1997).

49. R. Barthes, *S/Z*, trans. R. Miller (New York: Hill and Wang, 1974).

50. G. Deleuze and F. Guattari, *A Thousand Plateaus: Capitalism and Schizophrenia* (Minneapolis: University of Minnesota Press, 1987).

51. J.D. Bolter and R. Grusin, *Remediation: Understanding New Media* (Cambridge, Mass.: MIT Press, 1999).

52. Manovich, *The Language of New Media*, pp. 30–1.

53. R. Williams, *Television, Technology and Cultural Form* (London: Fontana, 1974); *Towards 2000* (London: Chatto and Windus, 1982).

54. S. Plant, 'On the mobile: the effects of mobile telephones on social and individual life', <http://www.motorola.com/mediacenter> (2001).

55. G. Myerson, *Heidegger, Habermas and the Mobile Phone* (Duxford: Icon Books, 2001).

56. See B. Winston, *Media Technology and Society: A History from the Telegraph to the Internet* (London: Routledge, 1998).
57. N. Perry, 'Ringing the changes: the cultural meanings of the telephone', in L. Goode and N. Zuberi (eds), *Media Studies in Aotearoa/New Zealand* (Auckland: Pearson Longman, 2004), pp. 158–60.
58. 'Listening otherwise: music miniaturised ',in R. Chow, *Writing Diaspora: Tactics of Intervention in Contemporary Cultural Studies* (Bloomington and Indianapolis: Indiana University Press, 1993). I'm indebted to Nabeel Zuberi for introducing me to this and other interesting perspectives on cultures of mobile devices.
59. S. Turkle, *Life on the Screen: Identity in the Age of the Internet* (New York: Simon and Schuster, 1995).
60. A. Balsamo, 'The virtual body in cyberspace', in D. Bell and B. Kennedy (eds), *The Cybercultures Reader* (London: Routledge, 2000), pp. 489–503.
61. W. Benjamin, 'The work of art in the age of mechanical reproduction', in *Illuminations* (London: Fontana, 1990 [1936]), pp. 211–44.

5   UNFINISHED PROJECTS: REFLEXIVE DEMOCRACY

1. U. Beck, 'The reinvention of politics: towards a theory of reflexive modernisation', in U. Beck, A. Giddens and S. Lash, *Reflexive Modernization* (Cambridge: Polity Press, 1994).
2. It may seem odd to invoke Anthony Giddens in a discourse that problematises 'Third Way' social democracy. I think, in fact, that the term 'Third Way' conceals more than it reveals, and although he has been associated with Tony Blair's UK government, it is too simplistic to call Giddens a spokesperson for Blairite Third Way politics. But whilst Giddens' ideas may be more radical than either the policies, aspirations or ideologies of the Blair government, I will go on to suggest that they may not be radical enough.
3. A. Giddens, *Beyond Left and Right: The Future of Radical Politics* (Cambridge: Polity Press, 1994), p. 95.
4. J.F. Lyotard, *The Postmodern Condition: A Report on Knowledge*, trans. G. Bennington and B. Massumi (Manchester: Manchester University Press, 1986 [1979]).
5. A. Giddens, *The Consequences of Modernity* (Cambridge: Polity Press, 1990), p. 84.
6. Ibid., pp. 135–7.
7. Ibid., p. 85.
8. Ibid., pp. 87–8.
9. Giddens, *Beyond Left and Right*, p. 94.
10. Ibid., pp. 95–6.
11. See B. Latour, *Politics of Nature: How to Bring the Sciences into Democracy*, trans. C. Porter (Cambridge, Mass.: Harvard University Press, 2004.)
12. See, for example, N. Stevenson (ed.), *Cultural Citizenship: Cosmopolitan Questions* (Maidenhead: Open University Press, 2003).
13. Giddens, *The Consequences of Modernity*, pp. 123–4.

14. S. Lash and J. Urry, *Economies of Signs and Space* (London: Sage, 1994), p. 39.
15. Giddens, *Beyond Left and Right*, pp. 90–1.
16. U. Beck, *Risk Society: Towards a New Modernity*, trans. M. Ritter (London: Sage, 1992 [1986]); *Ecological Politics in an Age of Risk*, trans. A. Weisz (Cambridge: Polity Press, 1995 [1988]).
17. Beck, *Risk Society*, pp. 21–2.
18. Ibid., p. 34.
19. Giddens, *Modernity and Self-Identity*, pp. 123–4; Giddens, *Beyond Left and Right*, pp. 220–3.
20. Beck, 'The reinvention of politics', pp. 6–7.
21. Z. Bauman, *Postmodern Ethics* (Oxford: Blackwell, 1993), pp. 196ff.
22. Beck, *Risk Society*, p. 71.
23. Ibid., p. 159.
24. Ibid., p. 157.
25. Ibid., p. 172.
26. Ibid., p. 60.
27. Ibid., p. 232.
28. Beck, 'The reinvention of politics', p. 28.
29. Beck, *Risk Society*, p. 234.
30. Giddens, *Beyond Left and Right*.
31. Ibid., pp. 252–3; Beck, *Risk Society*, p. 48.
32. Beck, *Risk Society*, p. 36.
33. J. Habermas, 'The new obscurity: the crisis of the welfare state and the exhaustion of utopian energies', in *The New Conservativism: Cultural Criticism and the Historians' Debate*, trans. S. Weber Nicholsen (Cambridge: Polity Press, p. 64).
34. J. Keane, *Democracy and Civil Society* (London: Verso, 1987), p. 15.
35. J. Habermas, *The Future of Human Nature* (Cambridge: Polity Press, 2003).
36. J. Derrida, *Specters of Marx: The State of the Debt, the Work of Mourning, and the New International*, trans. P. Kamuf (London: Routledge, 1994); J. Derrida, *Archive Fever: A Freudian Impression*, trans. E. Prenowitz (Chicago: University of Chicago Press, 1996); J.D. Peters, *Speaking into the Air: A History of the Idea of Communication* (Chicago: University of Chicago Press, 1999). Within this discourse, the impossibility of 'authentic' communications between the living and the dead functions as a model for the impossibility of authentic communications per se. It also looks at the prevalent cultural fascination for 'talking with the dead' manifested in literature, film, genealogy, historical archives and so forth, making the ironic suggestion that we can treat this impossibility as a productive force that gives rise to, rather than prevents, communication.
37. Habermas, 'The new obscurity', p. 51.

Bibliography

Adorno, T.W., *The Culture Industry: Selected Essays on Mass Culture*, ed. J.M. Bernstein (London: Routledge, 1991).

—— Albert, H., Dahrendorf, R., Habermas, J., Pilot, H. and Popper, K., *The Positivist Dispute in German Sociology*, trans. G. Adey and D. Frisby (London: Heinemann, 1977 [1969]).

Anderson, B., *Imagined Communities: Reflections on the Origin and Spread of Nationalism* (London: Verso, 1991).

Appadurai, A., *Modernity at Large: Cultural Dimensions of Globalization* (Minneapolis: University of Minnesota Press, 1996).

Baker, K., 'Defining the public sphere in eighteenth-century France: variations on a theme by Habermas', in Calhoun (ed.), *Habermas and the Public Sphere*.

Balsamo, A., 'The virtual body in cyberspace', in D. Bell and B. Kennedy (eds), *The Cybercultures Reader* (London: Routledge, 2000).

Barthes, R., *S/Z*, trans. R. Miller (New York: Hill and Wang, 1974).

Baudrillard, J., *In the Shadow of the Silent Majorities, or the End of the Social and Other Essays*, trans. P. Foss (New York: Semiotexte, 1983).

Bauman, Z., *Postmodern Ethics* (Oxford: Blackwell, 1993).

Beck, U., *Risk Society: Towards a New Modernity*, trans. M. Ritter (London: Sage, 1992 [1986]).

—— *Ecological Politics in an Age of Risk*, trans. A. Weisz (Cambridge: Polity Press, 1995 [1988]).

—— 'The reinvention of politics: towards a theory of reflexive modernisation', in U. Beck, A. Giddens and S. Lash, *Reflexive Modernization* (Cambridge: Polity Press, 1994).

Benjamin, W., 'The work of art in the age of mechanical reproduction', in *Illuminations* (London: Fontana, 1990 [1936]).

Blaug, R., *Democracy, Real and Ideal: Discourse Ethics and Radical Politics* (Albany: State University of New York Press, 1999).

Benhabib, S., *Situating the Self: Gender, Community and Postmodernism in Contemporary Ethics* (Cambridge: Polity Press, 1992).

Bolter, J.D. and Grusin, R., *Remediation: Understanding New Media* (Cambridge, Mass.: MIT Press, 1999).

Calhoun, C., 'Populist politics, communications media and large scale societal integration', *Sociological Theory*, vol. 6 (Fall, 1988).

—— (ed.), *Habermas and the Public Sphere* (Cambridge, Mass.: MIT Press, 1992).

Castells, M., *The Rise of the Network Society*, 2nd edn (Oxford: Blackwell, 2000).

Chow, R., *Writing Diaspora: Tactics of Intervention in Contemporary Cultural Studies* (Bloomington and Indianapolis: Indiana University Press, 1993).

Connery, B., 'IMHO: authority and egalitarian rhetoric in the virtual coffeehouse', in D. Porter (ed.), *Internet Culture* (London: Routledge, 1997).

Cronin, C. and de Greiff, P., 'Translators' introduction', in Habermas, *The Inclusion of the Other*.

Dahlgren, P. and Sparks, C. (eds), *Communication and Citizenship: Journalism and the Public Sphere* (London: Sage, 1991).

Deleuze, G. and Guattari, F., *A Thousand Plateaus: Capitalism and Schizophrenia* (Minneapolis: University of Minnesota Press, 1987).

Derrida, J., *Specters of Marx: The State of the Debt, the Work of Mourning, and the New International*, trans. P. Kamuf (London: Routledge, 1994).

—— *Archive Fever: a Freudian Impression*, trans. E. Prenowitz (Chicago: University of Chicago Press, 1996).

Eco, U., *The Role of the Reader: Explorations in the Semiotics of Texts* (Bloomington: Indiana University Press, 1984).

Eley, G., 'Nations, publics and political cultures: placing Habermas in the nineteenth century', in Calhoun (ed.), *Habermas and the Public Sphere*.

European Commission, *Convergence Green Paper: Working Document* <http://www.ispo.cec.be/convergencegp/gpworkdoc.html> (1998).

Fraser, N., 'Rethinking the public sphere: a contribution to the critique of actually existing democracy', in Calhoun (ed.), *Habermas and the Public Sphere*.

Garnham, N., 'The media and the public sphere', in Calhoun (ed.), *Habermas and the Public Sphere*.

Giddens, A., *The Consequences of Modernity* (Cambridge: Polity Press, 1990).

—— *Modernity and Self-Identity: Self and Society in the Late Modern Age* (Cambridge: Polity Press, 1991).

—— *Beyond Left and Right: The Future of Radical Politics* (Cambridge: Polity Press, 1994).

Gilligan, C., *In a Different Voice: Psychological Theory and Women's Development* (Cambridge, Mass.: Harvard University Press, 1982).

Gitlin, T., 'Public sphere or public sphericules?', in T. Liebes and J. Curran (eds), *Media, Ritual, Identity* (London: Routledge, 1998).

Golding, P. and Murdock, G., 'Culture, Communications and Political Economy', in J. Curran and M. Gurevitch (eds), *Mass Media and Society*, 2nd edn (London: Arnold, 1991).

Habermas, J., *The Structural Transformation of the Public Sphere: An Inquiry into a Category of Bourgeois Society*, trans. T. Burger (Cambridge: Polity Press, 1989 [1962]).

—— *Toward a Rational Society: Student Protest, Science and Politics*, trans. J. Shapiro (Cambridge: Polity Press, 1987 [1962]).

—— 'The scientisation of politics and public opinion', in *Toward a Rational Society*.

—— 'The university in a democracy', in *Toward a Rational Society*.

—— 'Technical progress and the social life-world', in *Toward a Rational Society*.

—— 'Technology and science as "ideology"', in *Toward a Rational Society*.

—— *Knowledge and Human Interests*, trans. J. Shapiro (Cambridge: Polity Press, 1987 [1968]).

—— *Legitimation Crisis* (London: Heinemann 1976).

—— *Communication and the Evolution of Society*, trans. T. McCarthy (Cambridge: Polity Press, 1984 [1976]).

—— *Philosophical and Political Profiles*, trans. F. Lawrence (London: Heinemann, 1983).

—— *The Theory of Communicative Action vol. 1: Reason and the Rationalisation of Society*, trans. T. McCarthy (Cambridge: Polity Press, 1991 [1981]).

—— *The Theory of Communicative Action vol. 2: Lifeworld and System: The Critique of Functionalist Reason*, trans. T. McCarthy (Cambridge: Polity Press, 1987 [1981]).

—— *Moral Consciousness and Communicative Action*, trans. C. Lenhardt and S. Weber Nicholsen (Cambridge: Polity Press, 1990 [1983]).

—— *The Philosophical Discourse of Modernity*, trans. F. Lawrence (Cambridge: Polity Press, 1987).

—— 'The new obscurity: the crisis of the welfare state and the exhaustion of utopian energies', in *The New Conservativism: Cultural Criticism and the Historians' Debate*, trans. S. Weber Nicholsen (Cambridge: Polity Press, 1989).

—— 'What does socialism mean today? The rectifying revolution and the need for new thinking on the Left', *New Left Review*, no. 183 (1990).

—— *Postmetaphysical Thinking: Philosophical Essays*, trans. W.M. Hohengarten (Cambridge, Mass.: MIT Press, 1992).

—— 'Further reflections on the public sphere', in Calhoun (ed.), *Habermas and the Public Sphere* (Cambridge, Mass.: MIT Press, 1992).

—— 'Concluding remarks', in Calhoun (ed.), *Habermas and the Public Sphere*.

—— *Between Facts and Norms: Contributions to a Discourse Theory of Law and Democracy*, trans. W. Rehg (Cambridge: Polity Press, 1996).

—— 'Postscript to *Between Facts and Norms*', in M. Deflem (ed.), *Habermas, Modernity and Law* (London: Sage, 1996).

—— *The Inclusion of the Other: Studies in Political Theory*, trans. C. Cronin and P. de Greiff (Cambridge, Mass.: MIT Press, 1998).

—— *The Future of Human Nature* (Cambridge: Polity Press, 2003).

Haraway, D., *Simians, Cyborgs and Women: The Reinvention of Nature* (New York: Routledge, 1991).

Held, D., 'Democracy and the new international order', in D. Archibugi and D. Held (eds), *Cosmopolitan Democracy: An Agenda for a New World Order* (Cambridge: Polity Press, 1995).

Hohendahl, P., 'Critical theory, public sphere and culture: Jürgen Habermas and his critics', *New German Critique*, vol. 16 (1979).

Holub, R., *Habermas: Critic in the Public Sphere* (London: Routledge, 1991).

Jay, M., 'Habermas and Modernism', in R. Bernstein (ed.), *Habermas and Modernity* (Cambridge: Polity Press, 1985).

Jameson, F., *Postmodernism, or the Cultural Logic of Late Capitalism* (London: Verso, 1990).

Katz, J., 'Birth of a digital nation', *Wired*, vol. 5.04 (1996).

Keane, J., *Democracy and Civil Society* (London: Verso, 1987).

—— *The Media and Democracy* (Cambridge: Polity Press, 1991).

Kellner, D., *Media Culture: Cultural Studies, Identity and Politics Between the Modern and the Postmodern* (London: Routledge, 1995).
—— 'Techno-politics, new technologies, and the new public spheres', <http://www.uta.edu/huma/illuminations> (1998).
Laclau, E., *Emancipation(s)* (London: Verso, 1996).
—— and Mouffe, C., *Hegemony and Socialist Strategy: Towards a Radical Democratic Politics* (London: Verso, 1985).
Landow, G.P., *Hypertext 2.0* (Baltimore: Johns Hopkins University Press, 1997).
Lash, S. and Urry, J., *Economies of Signs and Space* (London: Sage, 1994).
Latour, B., 'Whose cosmos, which cosmopolitics? Comments on the peace terms of Ulrich Beck', <http://www.ensmp.fr/~latour/articles/article/92-BECK-CK.html> (2004).
—— *Politics of Nature: How to Bring the Sciences into Democracy*, trans. C. Porter (Cambridge, Mass.: Harvard University Press, 2004).
Lunenfeld, P., *Snap to Grid: A User's Guide to Digital Arts, Media and Cultures* (Cambridge, Mass.: MIT Press, 2000).
Lyotard, J.F., *The Postmodern Condition: A Report on Knowledge*, trans. G. Bennington and B. Massumi (Manchester: Manchester University Press, 1986 [1979]).
Manovich, L., *The Language of New Media* (Cambridge, Mass.: MIT Press, 2001).
Marx, K., 'A Contribution to the Critique of Hegel's Philosophy of Right: Introduction' [1843–44] in *Early Writings*, trans. R. Livingstone and G. Benton (Harmondsworth: Penguin Books, 1992).
McLuhan, M., *Understanding Media: The Extensions of Man* (London: Routledge, 1994 [1964]).
Morley, D. and Robins, K., *Spaces of Identity: Global Media, Electronic Landscapes and Cultural Boundaries* (London: Routledge, 1995).
McCarthy, T., *The Critical Theory of Jürgen Habermas* (Cambridge: Polity Press, 1979).
Myerson, G., *Heidegger, Habermas and the Mobile Phone* (Duxford: Icon Books, 2001).
Negroponte, N., *Being Digital* (London: Coronet, 1996).
Negt, O. and Kluge, A., 'The public sphere and experience: selections', trans. P. Labanyi, *October*, no. 46 (Fall, 1988 [1972]).
Offe, C., *Contradictions of the Welfare State* (London: Hutchinson, 1984).
Perry, N., 'Ringing the changes: the cultural meanings of the telephone', in L. Goode and N. Zuberi (eds), *Media Studies in Aotearoa/New Zealand* (Auckland: Pearson Longman, 2004).
Peters, J.D., 'Distrust of representation: Habermas on the public sphere', *Media, Culture and Society*, vol. 15 (1993).
—— *Speaking into the Air: A History of the Idea of Communication* (Chicago: University of Chicago Press, 1999).
Plant, S., 'On the mobile: the effects of mobile telephones on social and individual life', <http://www.motorola.com/mediacenter> (2001).
Poster, M., *The Second Media Age* (Cambridge: Polity Press, 1995).

—— 'Cyberdemocracy: Internet and the Public Sphere', in D. Porter (ed.), *Internet Culture* (London: Routledge, 1997).

—— *What's the Matter with the Internet?* (Minneapolis: University of Minnesota Press, 2001).

Pfeufer Kahn, R., 'The problem of power in Habermas', *Human Studies*, vol. 11, no. 4 (1988).

Ray, L., *Rethinking Critical Theory: Emancipation in the Age of Social Movements* (London: Sage, 1993).

Rheingold, H., *Virtual Community: Finding Connection in a Computerized World* (London: Vintage, 1993).

Ryan, M., 'Gender and public access: women's politics in nineteenth-century America', in Calhoun (ed.), *Habermas and the Public Sphere*.

Said, E., *Culture and Imperialism* (London: Vintage, 1994).

Scanell, P., 'Public service broadcasting and modern public life', in P. Scannell et al. (eds), *Culture and Power* (London: Sage, 1991).

—— 'Public service broadcasting: the history of a concept', in A. Goodwin and G. Whannel (eds), *Understanding Television* (London: Routledge, 1992).

Schiller, D., *Digital Capitalism: Networking the Global Market System* (Cambridge, Mass.: MIT Press, 1999).

Schiller, H., 'The global information highway: project for an ungovernable world', in J. Brook and I. Boal (eds), *Resisting the Virtual Life: The Culture and Politics of Information* (San Francisco: City Light Books, 1995).

Schlesinger, P., 'Europe's contradictory communicative space', *Dædalus*, vol. 123, no. 2 (1994).

Sennett, R., *The Fall of Public Man* (London: Faber and Faber, 1986 [1977]).

Stevenson, N., *Understanding Media Cultures: Social Theory and Mass Communication* (London: Sage 1995).

—— (ed.), *Cultural Citizenship: Cosmopolitan Questions* (Maidenhead: Open University Press, 2003).

Thompson, E.P. *The Making of the English Working Class* (Harmondsworth: Penguin, 1968).

Thompson, J.B., *Ideology and Modern Culture: Critical Theory in the Era of Mass Communication* (Cambridge: Polity Press, 1990).

—— 'The theory of the public sphere', *Theory, Culture and Society*, vol. 10, no. 3 (1993).

—— 'Social theory and the media', in D. Crowley and D. Mitchell (eds), *Communication Theory Today* (Cambridge: Polity Press, 1994).

—— *The Media and Modernity: A Social Theory of the Media* (Cambridge: Polity Press, 1995).

Turkle, S., *Life on the Screen: Identity in the Age of the Internet* (New York: Simon and Schuster, 1995).

Wark, M., *Virtual Geography: Living with Global Media Events* (Bloomington: Indiana University Press, 1994).

Warner, M., 'The mass public and the mass subject', in B. Robbins (ed.), *The Phantom Public Sphere* (Minneapolis: University of Minnesota Press, 1993).

Williams, R., *Television, Technology and Cultural Form* (London: Fontana, 1974).

—— *Towards 2000* (London: Chatto and Windus, 1982).

Winston, B., *Media Technology and Society: A History from the Telegraph to the Internet* (London: Routledge, 1998).

Zaret, D., 'Religion, science, and printing in the public spheres in seventeenth-century England', in Calhoun (ed.), *Habermas and the Public Sphere*.

Index

DATE DUE